Ivan Misner's insightful work explores h[...]
similarities and differences between the s[...]
for your business relationships. Don't let your gender hinder
your networking ability!

—HARVEY MACKAY, AUTHOR OF THE #1 *NEW YORK TIMES* BESTSELLER
SWIM WITH THE SHARKS WITHOUT BEING EATEN ALIVE

Networking is about relationships, plain and simple. Understanding
the opposite sex in a new and positive light is the key to building
lasting business relationships for increasing success. The sooner
you read *Business Networking and Sex*, the sooner you will
achieve success.

—JOHN GRAY, BESTSELLING AUTHOR OF
MEN ARE FROM MARS AND WOMEN ARE FROM VENUS

Impeccably researched, backed up by hard-hitting statistics, filled with
laugh-out-loud humor, and packed with cutting-edge information
on how to take your networking results to the next level—*Business
Networking and Sex* is the must-have networking guide
for the 21st century.

—JACK CANFIELD, BESTSELLING AUTHOR OF THE
CHICKEN SOUP SERIES AND *THE SUCCESS PRINCIPLES*

Wow! This book shows you how to build and maintain quality
business networking contacts with the other
50 percent of the population.

—BRIAN TRACY, AUTHOR OF *THE POWER OF CHARM*

I've never been one to mix business with pleasure but with this book
it's impossible not to—whether you're reading for business or
reading for pleasure, *Business Networking and Sex* delivers a
thoroughly informative, thoroughly entertaining
experience from cover to cover.

—LISA NICHOLS, FEATURED TEACHER IN *THE SECRET* AND
AUTHOR OF *NO MATTER WHAT!*

There's something I love about Ivan Misner's approach to business—he's so focused! In this wonderful new book he takes yet another new and novel look at networking, and tells us why it works, how it works, and why it is so necessary for all of us to take it as seriously as we do the most important functions in our businesses . . . or live to pay the price. Read this book, and send a copy to a friend. Important stuff for all of us determined to grow in this difficult, difficult world. Thank you, Ivan, for your focus. We all need it!

—MICHAEL E. GERBER, AUTHOR OF THE WORLD'S #1 SMALL BUSINESS BOOK, *THE E-MYTH: WHY MOST BUSINESSES DON'T WORK AND WHAT TO DO ABOUT IT*

You've heard the phrase "sex sells," but have you ever heard anyone explain how to sell to the opposite sex? No matter what your product or service, your business depends on sales and increased sales depend on how effective you are at building relationships and networking—with women and men alike. *Business Networking and Sex* outlines the key similarities and differences between the genders when it comes to networking so you'll never have to guess again about the best way to sell to the opposite sex.

—DR. TONY ALESSANDRA, AUTHOR OF *THE PLATINUM RULE* AND *NON-MANIPULATIVE SELLING*

A wonderfully revealing look at the way men and women interact in the world of business and beyond.

—MARCI SHIMOFF, *NEW YORK TIMES* BESTSELLING AUTHOR OF *HAPPY FOR NO REASON* AND *LOVE FOR NO REASON*

HELLO
my name is

Business Networking
AND SEX

(not what you think)

Ivan Misner, Ph.D.   Hazel M. Walker   Frank J. De Raffele Jr.

EP
Entrepreneur.
Press

Entrepreneur Press, Publisher
Cover design: Andrew Welyczko
Composition and production: Eliot House Productions

This publication is designed to provide accurate and authoritative information
in regard to the subject matter covered. It is sold with the understanding that the
publisher is not engaged in rendering legal, accounting, or other professional services. If legal advice or other expert assistance is required, the services of a competent professional person should be sought.

Library of Congress Cataloging-in-Publication Data
Misner, Ivan R., 1956–.
　　　　Business networking and sex : not what you think! / by Ivan Misner,
　　Frank J. DeRaffele, Jr., and Hazel Walker.
　　　　　　p.　cm.
　　　　　　Includes bibliographical references.
　　　　　　ISBN-13: 978-1-59918-424-1
　　　　　　ISBN-10: 1-59918-424-9 (alk. paper)
　　　　　　1. Business networks. 2. Sexism. 3. Sex (Psychology) I. DeRaffele, Frank J.
　　II. Walker, Hazel. III. Title.
　　HD69.S8M564 2012
　　650.1'3—dc23　　　　　　　　　　　　　　　　2011034173

Printed in the United States of America

16 15 14 13 12　　　　　　　　　　　　　　　　10 9 8 7 6 5 4 3 2 1

Dedication

This book is dedicated with love to my bride
of 23 years, Elisabeth, who often says,
"You make the living and I'll make the living worthwhile"
. . . and she does with each passing day.

—Ivan Misner, Ph.D.

I dedicate this book to my three girls:
Crystal, Jacqueline and Candace.
The loves of my life.

—Frank De Raffele

I dedicate this book, to my team who managed the business
while I wrote a book, to my friends who cheered me on.
Most of all to my family, who believe in me and are
always there to lend a hand. I love you all.

—Hazel Walker

Contents

WARNING

This book is about sex.

(OK, it's really about gender—but the warning is still valid.)

This book may make you angry!

We will talk about issues that are controversial.

It will likely push some buttons.

Worst of all, there is some statistical analysis involved!

Be warned and be brave.

Take a deep breath. You're an adult.

You can handle it . . . we hope.

Meet the Authors

Ivan Misner, Ph.D., alias, "The Survey Says . . ."

Dr. Ivan Misner is the Founder and Chairman of BNI, the world's largest business networking organization. BNI was founded in 1985 and has more than 6,000 chapters throughout every populated continent of the world. Every year, BNI generates millions of referrals resulting in billions of dollars' worth of business for its members.

Dr. Misner's Ph.D. is from the University of Southern California. He is a *New York Times* bestselling author, having written 16 books, including his number-one bestseller, *Networking Like a Pro*. He is a monthly columnist for www.Entrepreneur.com and a senior partner of the Referral Institute, a global referral training company. In addition, he has taught business management and social capital courses at several universities in the United States.

Called the "Father of Modern Networking" by CNN and the "Networking Guru" by *Entrepreneur* magazine, Dr. Misner is considered to be one of the world's leading experts on business networking and is a keynote speaker for major corporations and associations throughout the world. He has been featured in the the *Los Angeles Times, The Wall Street Journal*, and *The New York Times*, as well as numerous TV and radio shows including CNN, CNBC, and the BBC in London.

Dr. Misner is on the board of trustees for the University of La Verne. He is also the founder of the BNI–Misner Charitable Foundation and was recently named "Humanitarian of the Year" by the Red Cross. He is married and lives with his wife, Beth, and their three children in Claremont, California. He also wears the hats of amateur magician and karate black belt in his spare time.

♂ Frank J. De Raffele Jr., alias, "He Says"

Frank began his spirited entrepreneurial journey at age 18 when he incorporated his first business and then went on to establish Innovative Video Productions fresh out of college, producing a fitness video series featured nationally through Herman's Sporting Goods, American Express Mailers, and the Sharper Image Catalog.

As a producer, his endeavors included sports-TV shows and commercials for clients such as Liberty Mutual, Ford, and the PGA, as well as serving as part of the news crew team at ABC Television and production team on the soap opera *One Life to Live*. These prepped him for the creation of a dynamic production, Entrepreneurial Excellence Radio Show Inc., on which he exposes entrepreneurs to the information they need for success.

As founder and president of Entrepreneurial Excellence Worldwide Inc., and through the ProActive Leadership Center, Frank's seminars motivate professionals globally. His presentations have been translated into Japanese, Chinese, German, French, and Dutch.

His competitive flair touches all that he does and drove him to compete in the Golden Gloves Boxing trials at age 30, as well as earn a sixth-degree black belt in Okinawan Goju Ryu Karate.

♀ Hazel M. Walker, alias, "She Says"

When Hazel found herself the reluctant owner of an insurance agency, having zero experience in either the insurance field or being a business owner, she knew she had a lot to learn fast. In the process she learned that she loved networking and connecting others. As a BNI and Referral Institute franchise owner, Hazel has been teaching professionals how to grow their businesses through the art of referral for 13 years. Her multiple contributing-author projects, Toastmaster Bronze status, and membership in the National Speakers Association all add to the rich array of experiences she draws on for the wisdom of this book.

Her volunteerism includes Big Brothers Big Sisters, Business Ownership Initiative, the Warren Township PTA, and the Indiana State PTA, at which she earned the Indiana State PTA Lifetime Membership Award.

Inspired by her children, Hazel's deep curiosity and yearning to learn attracts her to global travel and adventure. Her special interests include learning about craft beers, hosting tastings, and pairing beers for women who want to learn more. She has a passion for helping women business owners create businesses that they love, allowing them to live the life they choose.

■ ■ ■

Lucky you! You've got three seasoned guides to escort you step by step through the rocky terrain of gender communication conflict, in an easy-to-absorb system. Each chapter presents quantitative survey respondents' opinions and quotes, interpreted by me (The Survey), and a spirited discussion of these sometimes contradictory, sometimes surprising findings by He (Frank) and She (Hazel).

He and She will help you interpret difficult subject matter through the very important differing perspectives of each gender. The supplemental data, combined with Hazel and Frank's brutal honesty and my voice of reason, make for a bumpy, if not thrilling, ride. Fasten your seatbelts, ladies and gents: It's going to be wild!

Introduction

 The Survey Says . . .

Over a four-year period, more than 12,000 businesspeople participated in a study focused around 25 simple questions. Beyond irritating you, the answers may also make you excited and motivated to learn.

As we sift through the statistical analysis, the last thing you'll do is yawn; rather, you'll probably be recalling your own emotionally loaded responses to the electrical storms that occur between the genders as we struggle to understand one another within the quickly evolving and competitive arena of business.

Be brave! You can handle it. Take a deep breath, and when you feel like giving one of our authors or study subjects a piece of your mind, bite your lip and keep reading, for when all is said and done, you'll walk away with something equivalent to a graduate degree in "network speak for the other sex."

You may wonder what the impetus was for a study on business, networking, and sex. Having run the world's largest business networking organization for almost three decades, it would be an understatement to say that I've witnessed men and women experience some networking-specific communication challenges. Hidden in the glitches are often misleading assumptions about each gender that beg to be investigated, unveiled, and understood.

The results of our study unearthed astounding breakthroughs that will change the habits and results of your face-to-face networking process.

In a desire to understand the communication roadblocks that occur between women and men in the networking process, our team of authors focused on combining their personal networking experiences with the data and interpreting its greater meaning for readers.

Finally, the findings are translated into action steps for each gender with which to shape their networking style so that they may take advantage of the full potential that building social capital has to offer.

My objective is to offer the data in a gender-neutral presentation; just interpreting the study findings through the lens of decades of long, seasoned, cross-cultural experience. I do my best to stay away from speaking for my gender or giving opinions on the female gender. Believe me, you'll get more than enough gender-slanted opinions, interpretations, jabs, and strong suggestions from She and He, represented by Hazel and Frank.

♂ He Says . . .
We Want the Same Things but Get Them Differently

It's interesting that our study revealed two very distinct facts, seemingly at odds with one another. The first is that both men and women want to get business from networking and are willing to work hard to get it. The second is that we seem to make things so difficult for ourselves by only networking in the style our own gender prefers and understands. This is as counterproductive as a heterosexual marriage based either on only what the man wants, or only what the woman wants. If they both want to stay married they quickly figure out what it takes to make the other person happy and do it.

Speaking of Sex

You may be wondering what sex has to do with networking. You may also be excited to learn how to use your sexual prowess to influence business deals and, around the office, to get things to go the way you'd like. Get your mind out of the gutter! Sorry to burst your bubble, but this book is really more about gender than sex, but who's going to do a double take at the bookstore for the title *Business, Networking, and Gender*? Do I hear crickets chirping? That's exactly why we used the more scintillating title, *Business Networking and Sex*. Not many people walk around thinking about gender, but many people think many times a day about, well, you know.

Do You Make the Cut?

Are you ready to be made fun of, stereotyped, discounted, insulted, and blamed for what someone else has done? Do you have the ability to take a good, hard look at your own behavior and make changes that may be uncomfortable at first? Can you laugh at yourself and stop taking everything so seriously for a little while? Then read on. The rewards are great.

Do we really like to make things difficult for ourselves? Is the problem that our culturally gender-specific values and sexual brain chemistry actually handicap us from working well together? Give me a break! This is a cop-out. I do have another question, though, for which I must apologize ahead of time. Are we men really idiots? Absolutely. In fact, our study confirms what people have known for a long time, and that is that sometimes men behave as pigs. Here are a couple of quotes from our study about professional men in networking situations:

> *Not to be sexist, but the hot businesswoman will always draw a larger crowd at networking functions because men assume that giving business to her will make her like him.*

> *In a structured networking group, I find having female members there very beneficial because it ensures that the men are more present and polite.*

Are we really this stupid and shallow? Apparently some of us are, and all it takes is a few to create a reputation. It's pretty sad that we need females in the room to make us behave in a civilized manner. Sheesh. Ladies, on behalf of men everywhere, I apologize. I know I'll feel the urge to do that frequently throughout the book, but this will be the one and only time for the sake of space and sanity.

One of those continually agitating issues between genders that lands us guys in the doghouse over and over is the old, classic conundrum that I like to call, "What'd I say?!" Men, I'm sure you know the feeling of trying to prepare your words, rehearsing them over and over to remove any offensive bits and head trouble off at the pass, and then still somehow wind up saying the wrong thing to the woman in your life. Of course there are the many times I've also had communication problems with female coworkers. I've had countless women tell me how offended or put off they were by what some guy at a networking meeting said, yet they said nothing at the time to him, but quietly decided to either never use his service or business, or give him referrals.

The question is, has there ever been a long stretch of time in your life, guys, in which you've not offended or been misunderstood by women? No, of course not. What this means is that we are all losing a portion of our potential to do business with women because of this. The fact that almost half of the world's population is female should provide great motivation for us to get this problem solved!

This is the goal of the pages ahead. Because we make important, money-related decisions based on our assessments of facial expressions, gestures, tone, manners, and even smell, the face-to-face networking process is an opportunity for each gender to learn how to please the other. To grow as a business culture we must keep up with gender-specific communication styles and preferences. This means adapting to expected behavior, much like when traveling in a foreign land and observing its customs to make for a smooth vacation (not to mention to avoid landing in jail).

 ## She Says . . .
It's Especially Important for Women

A recent poll showed that 41.4 percent of businesses count on referrals for more than 80 percent of their sales. Furthermore, the U.S. Bureau of Labor Statistics finds that only 5 percent of job seekers obtain employment through the open job market, meaning primarily online and printed help-wanted ads. Another 24 percent get jobs by cold-calling companies directly. Twenty-three percent have success through employment agencies, college career-service offices, and executive search firms. The remaining 48 percent obtain their jobs through referrals. How do these work and business seekers get that word-of-mouth cycle to work for them? Face-to-face networking!

Not only does networking play a major role in growing a powerful business, but it also paves the way for a happy and secure life. Surely, anyone can see the benefits of having a pool of amiable friends and associates ready to look out for them and send good things their way. Today, the abundance of related training media on word-of-mouth techniques is vast. People are hungry for knowledge about how to connect to others in a magnetic way that can change their lives. Now more than ever, men and women need to harness this training to hit the ground running and gain the mandatory business edge for thriving within our current economy's competitive markets.

What Are We Here For?

"Men seem to be more hesitant to build deep relationships and women tend to focus on pretty much everything else but business," wrote one of our survey respondents. This represents the conflicting thinking styles that make both genders in the same room wonder if they were really at the same event. It is the core reason why there are so many other conflicts in thinking and communication between the two.

If each sex is more skilled or drawn to different aspects of socializing, doesn't it seem that we can help one another with our resumes of respective natural talents? Helping women excel professionally is important, and if they have open minds and can handle the truth, I feel there is room for change and positive growth out of the comfortable ways that may be holding them back.

Though guys may act boorish and offensive at times, women need to really want to understand them. Yes, men can be pigs, but women play a bit part that enables men to continue that behavior, without even realizing it. How many times have you been offended by an off-color comment, yet said nothing and just sulked away? Have you ever been ignored, discounted, or rudely referred to, and instead of speaking your mind, just pouted and vowed never to give the guy any business?

Have you ever worn a sexy outfit to a business function and then felt offended that no one was taking you seriously, or worse yet, asking you out on dates rather than listening to your business ideas?

Mars vs. Venus

Dr. John Gray summed it up for all of us when he wrote his famous book, *Men Are from Mars, Women Are from Venus*. But business networking is just business networking, so it should be pretty straightforward, right? If we all have been reading the latest books on relating between the sexes and partaking in the most current networking training, then we should all be on the same page, right? You'd think so, but nothing could be farther from the truth. After working for years with businesspeople all over the world, it is clear that though they all want similar outcomes, their methods and communication styles are very different, which can cause endless problems and lost capital.

It really doesn't matter if you're "just" an employee with a secure job or a business owner looking to build up your empire. Knowing how to relate to both sexes will allow you to build a diverse network that can ultimately help connect you when you are looking for a new job, or connect your existing business to better products, skilled people, or more referred prospects. The best insurance you can take out on both personal and professional future is to network before you actually need anything. Think of the act of networking as building a huge, detailed net over time that will catch all kinds of great treasures, including you, if you fall.

BUSINESS-BUILDING MANTRA

Build your network before you need it and your "net" will "work" for you.

Now let's get started! There's a lot to learn.

The Exception Becomes the Perception

 The Survey Says . . .
Everyone Wants to Get Along

The realm of business today is global, not just local or national. When we set out to discover what people thought about business networking, we focused on businesspeople, but in a broad cross-section of the world. Over a three-year period, more than 12,000 businesspeople from every populated continent in the world participated in a survey about gender and business networking, the most comprehensive survey of its kind ever conducted. The survey was split almost evenly between men and women (50.2 percent men and 49.8 percent women). In their answers to the objective questions, men and women were not light years apart, as might have been expected. They mostly agreed, often quite closely, on the practices, values, and experiences of networking. The differences were oftentimes small, although statistically significant. No controversy there.

Then came a little surprise.

The final question on the survey was an open-ended one:

Do you have any story about networking between men and women that you would like to submit for possible use in the book? If so, please describe.

Nearly 1,000 participants responded. And what stories!

When given the opportunity to say something personal about their networking experiences, 545 women and 403 men revealed strikingly different perceptions. Despite their fairly close agreement on the objective questions, male and female businesspeople seemed to live in two different worlds. Many of the women wrote of feeling undervalued, intimidated, ignored, overshadowed, or patronized. Others told of sexual harassment, as shown here:

I sometimes feel as a woman it is hard to be taken seriously by some of the businessmen.

As a young marketer, any time I approached a member of the opposite sex, even when dressed conservatively and speaking only about business, they thought I was interested in dating. I didn't get too far with business.

One of the first "gentlemen" I met said, "Sorry, I didn't catch your name, I was too busy staring at your breasts."

Some men had negative things to say about the women they met and worked with, shown in the comments below:

I can recall a particular woman that would frequently attend networking meetings dressed for attention. This made men at the event who were attending with their spouses feel very uncomfortable.

When networking with women I find myself trying not to offend.

On the other hand, most of the men and many of the women gave positive responses. Some women even expressed a preference for working with men:

I actually feel more comfortable networking with the opposite sex. I feel women working with women are more competitive.

I especially like working with men. It's more direct with less "fluff."

Similarly, quite a few of the men said they enjoyed working with women:

As a male it is easier for me to network with a female. With women there's no ego issue.

I feel women are better networkers. Sometimes we men are more interested in handing out cards and talking business while women are more intuitive and like to listen. I always get more responses from women after I meet them at a social or business function.

However, almost all the respondents, even those who had positive comments, told us how differently they viewed men and women approaching the art of networking. Most seemed to agree that in networking situations, men were more focused on business and women on relationships.

As a sales trainer, I've noticed that men ask for the sale much more readily than do women, who need additional coaching in this area. I've witnessed this phenomenon for years.

It may sound sexist and completely contrary to all equal opportunity laws, but if I wasn't able and willing to be flirtatious with people, I don't think I'd be as successful as I am.

In their comments, men often cited the different networking styles of men and women but, on the whole, felt women did as good a job networking as men, or better. Their difficulties with women had mostly to do with not wanting to appear sexist.

Why did the opportunity to comment about the gender differences unleash such a strikingly different torrent of opinion?

In a phrase, we believe: The exception becomes the perception.

Most women don't put up sexy photos on their websites. Most men don't behave like frat boys. But it's the few who do that stand out. They give us the impression that there's a lot more of that sort of thing going on out there.

In our personal experience, if you ask individual men and women to think it over for a few minutes and then summarize in a single sentence how they feel about networking with the opposite sex, the vast majority of responses will sound something like this:

To me, people are people and gender doesn't play a large role. A person's attitude, competence, and interest in relationship building as opposed to selling are the attributes I look for when networking. In my business, valuable relationships with both men and women have been formed by paying attention to those attributes.

Then why were such a high percentage of the comments about the other sex, on both sides of the aisle, so negative? Because bad news travels faster than good news. (Remember the old saying? "Good news can wait but bad news will hunt you down.")

So although very few women report having any problems themselves, they have the perception that problems are very common because they've heard about them through the grapevine (or the internet). The same goes for men. They like networking with women and rarely encounter problems, but hear stories from somewhere else, often second- or third-hand, about women who are oversensitive to jokes or innocent comments or who imagine they're being discriminated against. They also hear about women who dress provocatively and women who won't network with men.

If this is the case, why did men and women give similar answers to many of the questions? Why are they in almost complete agreement on many of the issues about networking, including networking with the opposite sex?

Both the men and women in the survey are strongly committed to networking. They believe in it, practice it regularly, and look for ways to improve their networking-related skills. It works for them. The fact that difficulties arise doesn't alter their commitment to it. For the most part, men and women have similar goals for their networking efforts: They want to build their business. This similarity seems to compress some of the common differences that are expressed between the genders.

So when a problem arises and gets in the way of good networking, good businesspeople look for solutions.

HARDWIRED FOR SURVIVAL

Perhaps, by some distant hardwiring for survival, our species defaulted to remembering the negative. A recent Association for Psychological Science study reports Boston College psychologist Elizabeth Kensinger's study of the brain's strong preference for negative memories, explaining that our memories retain the most negative, dramatic details of an event to "at some point save our lives by guiding our actions and allowing us to plan for similar future occurrences."

If most networkers share this basically positive feeling about networking with the opposite sex, then why were there also so many negative comments in the final "tell us a networking story" part of our study? Bad news travels faster than good news because it is sensational. This is the same reason people slow down on the highway to stare at a grisly car accident, or tune into the news to sample the parade of violence and societal conflict that the less fortunate of our species has to offer.

Our deep-rooted survival skills may be storing negative information to save us from making those mistakes in our own lives. The residual purpose of collecting negative data may have run its course and left us with a strange, unanswered attention to the negative. The belief that the human appendix used to be for digesting bits of wood and now serves no purpose comes to mind. Who eats wood anymore, now that we are upright and frequent the salad bar at Whole Foods? Still, the appendix is there and can lead to problems.

Though very few women report having experienced their own problems, they have the perception that problems are common, through the grapevine effect. The same goes for men, each sex passing information speedily by way of the internet or gossip. They each enjoy networking with the other and rarely encounter problems, but hear second- and third-hand stories of worst-case scenarios.

Oh, how the stories circulate, from women who are overly sensitive to jokes and innocent comments to those who dress provocatively while complaining men are looking at their breasts and only work in female groups. And the numbers of men who are just trolling for dates under the guise of networking or making disrespectful, lewd remarks are endless. Or are they?

If this were actually a realistic representation of what's going on, why are men and women in almost total agreement about their true feelings regarding networking with the opposite sex? We've got two ways of phrasing a question. One is "How do you feel about networking with the opposite sex?" and the other is "Will you tell me a story about networking?"

It's possible that both feelings exist simultaneously for these survey participants, all of whom are dedicated networkers. Because everyone responding to this survey is already a dedicated professional, strongly committed to networking, they may just see these blips in professional behavior as challenges to be overcome. If one overall enjoys an experience and benefits from it, the fact that a small part of it is broken may just stimulate the desire to problem solve or repair the weakness, rather than changing one's entire opinion of it.

These responses show some of the willingness to problem solve and work through gender glitches:

As a female in a highly male-dominated industry, I sometimes find that men do not trust my competency level. I often bring a man with me to nod to everything I say. This works very well.

I find that if you bring someone with you of the opposite sex, you can more effectively work with that sex when they might otherwise feel uncomfortable. The person you are trying to get to know will feel more at ease when there is someone of their gender in the mix.

There was an instant shift in my networking responses once I donned my wedding ring. Suddenly the men I connected with focused on business more than men in the past had. When I didn't have the ring on men would say things like, "Let's have lunch first, then we'll talk about doing business." Married or unmarried, there was much more of a focus on socializing than building a professional relationship. It should take a few months of me reminding them about business before they'd commit to making an office appointment. As soon as the word of my marriage spread, men I had already connected to during networking now brought up the referrals I mentioned and wanted to act on them. It was so refreshing.

Hearing about worst-case scenarios is educational. The benefit of bad news circulating quickly is that we can afford an omniscient view and develop strategies to prepare for the worst. Why prepare for extreme circumstances? It can only help you.

The keen business professional is one who anticipates problems and is ready to act. Upon hearing of an unfortunate networking situation, one can come up with a solution while digesting the problem, and preemptively apply that to all situations as an insurance policy against grief. Most intelligent people get into their cars and immediately fasten their seat belts because, while the chances of getting into an accident or getting a ticket are low in comparison to how many times we drive, it can't hurt, is easy to do, and protects us from the worst-case scenario.

Yes, the perceived number of communication problems in mixed-company networking sessions is higher than the reality, but to be forewarned is to be forearmed. A savvy professional prepares for problem solving in advance, which is preventive medicine, or insurance for success. By heading off conflict at the pass you'll bolster group confidence, use time more efficiently, and be able to focus on the

GENDER DOS AND DON'TS

I f you want to improve your networking results, we have some advice for you, derived from the many responses in our study.

Some of the things men can do to avoid being perceived as sexist are:

- Maintain eye contact with women during conversation
- Stick to conversing about business
- Don't get too personal

To stop unwelcome advances from men, women should:

- Dress professionally
- Have a firm handshake, and be professional
- Under no circumstances flirt

matters at hand, rather than tying up your mind and emotions with squirmy social transgressions.

Once in a while, strong measures are required, and being ready makes all the difference in the world, as shown in this woman's story:

Generally, networking between men and women is trouble-free, however, just before one of our breakfast meetings started, I felt someone squeeze my behind. I turned around to find the offender looking very satisfied with himself, obviously trying to impress the two men standing next to him. This man was known for cramming innuendo into every possible conversation. I turned around and said, "Well &^%!!" I then went to my seat, thinking about how strange it was that we all appeared to be very grown-up professionals, yet this kind of thing was happening. Far from impressing his colleagues, he never did it to me or, as far as I witnessed, any other woman in our group again.

♂ He Says . . .
The X Perception Principle

You may remember hearing about the Pareto Principle, also known as the 80/20 rule. Usually this refers to the concept that 80 percent of the people do 20 percent of the work, within a business context. It also translates as spending 80 percent of your time on 20 percent of your clients, because only 20 percent of your clients are the ones that bring in the lion's share of profits. The remaining 80 are not as profitable.

I'd like to introduce you to my own concept: The X Perception Principle, also known as the 98/2 rule. Two percent of the population in each demographic creates a reputation for the remaining 98 percent. Does that seem fair? A chain is only as strong as its weakest link. In other words, the idiots making a scene, displaying notably poor judgment in social situations, ruin it for the rest of us. Hello, brethren, my male tribe, old chums—do you hear me? Good grief. That's quite a burden for the rest of us to shoulder.

That 2 percent of us who stare at women's chests during networking give them the impression that all of us are perverts. Hey, I know that it's just a scientific fact that we as a group tend to think about sex about every five seconds, but what is not a scientific fact is lack of control over our outward actions. If every man who thought about looking at a woman's chest actually did so, we'd probably have to rewind to caveman times for a glimpse at our achievements.

She Comments . . .

I can just imagine all the car accidents, botched surgeries, and fumbled footballs.

He Responds . . .

The fact is that some of us do sneak a peek now and then, but we're not stupid enough to actually get caught! This is not acceptable behavior. Any man in his right mind knows that there are no benefits and only disadvantages to being caught ogling in a business situation. For those of you who beg to differ, I suggest you stop watching those racy movies, because this is real life and we are multidimensional human beings dealing with one another, not paper cutouts.

I personally would appreciate a little camaraderie out there, a united front, or willingness to take on a little responsibility knowing that each of us out there is representing the whole male group. It's no wonder there are so many communication glitches and that we're prejudged when the 2 percent of cads out there is performing their nonstop jerk cabaret. Can you think of men that do this in any of the groups you belong to? I can. Knock it off, guys!

Religious affiliation, race, gender, sexual preference, and nationality are a few of the areas that fall victim to preconceived stereotypical notions because of the 2 percent exception creating a public caricature to represent the remaining 98 percent. It is unfortunate. One of the things we can do to influence positive ideas about our own gender is to both assess individuals on a case-by-case basis and act in a way we can be proud of to represent our tribe.

A Strange but True Tale of Misrepresentation

I've always known how important it is to dress for success, but I didn't realize the full ramifications of completely ignoring this rule until I met Poster Boy. I arrived at a business meeting, through my referral business, snappily dressed in a suit and tie, looking pretty good, I might add. I remember being impressed with the attendees because of their level of professionalism, friendliness, and commitment to networking.

Then I met HIM. The Poster Child of the time-old quandary of whether or not to judge a book by its cover. This giant, lumbering guy was so inappropriately dressed that I'm not even sure if he'd pass inspection at the beach. From the tips of his threadbare, holey Keds sneakers to the top of his unkempt Young Frankenstein mop, each detail along the way screamed, "I've been living in a cave for 20 years!" As if the blatantly visible hairy flanks and armpits gaping from his low-slung, flapping tank top weren't enough, tufts of back fur begging to be mown perfectly complemented the wrinkled shorts he'd apparently gotten from the bottom of his clothes hamper. This noticeably dampened my appetite for breakfast as well as deeply puzzled me because of his articulate, engaging conversational skills and obvious competency as a financial planner. It just didn't go with the train-wreck look he was projecting. The inside didn't match the outside.

Most male business professionals seem to understand what the respectable, appropriate dress codes are for their field. Not everyone is required to wear a suit and tie; rather, within each profession there is a standard that everyone adheres to (or should) that includes the uniform details of that profession. Roofers generally show up to give homeowners estimates dressed in something casual, but clean, that will allow them to climb up onto the roof and give their bid. It would seem inappropriate, and even shady, if a roofer showed up in this situation wearing a suit, wouldn't it? Other manual labor professionals dress appropriately for the work they'll be doing, whether it be jackhammering, trimming trees, or collecting your garbage. A banker helping customers set up loans doesn't show up for work in exercise gear. You get the point, but it's amazing that some people just don't.

People gravitate toward winners, and those winners win partially because they've observed a set of details that make people feel comfortable and secure. One of the ways to create an image that shows you've got your act together is to dress the way you'd like people to see you. Accept that humans are extremely visual animals and that we judge by what we see.

To inspire people to give you their money, which is the end goal in business, you've got to show them with the way you look and conduct yourself that this is a smart thing for them to do. Think of dressing well and observing social courtesies as earning your sale.

Men, listen up for some extra insight on this. Women in particular notice every detail in your attire, and will remember it for a very long time. How many times have you heard a couple reminisce about the first day they met and notice that the woman remembers exactly what both of them were wearing that day? If you want to impress everyone, dress for the female audience, and you can't go wrong. Pay fantastic attention to detail to capture your female audience, for they'll remember whether or not your suit matched your tie, if your shoes were polished, and if your suit sleeves were tailored to the right length.

Let's remember the women in our lives, guys, and their dressing process. When there's an upscale event coming up, the cycle begins. It starts with an hours-, days- or even weeks-long shopping bonanza for the perfect dress, and only ends when the pursuit of the matching shoes and jewelry yields a perfect score. Then comes the review: Scrutinizing model sessions in front of the mirror, turning this way and that, comparing it to other dresses, will have her asking you your opinion on whether it makes her look fat, outdated, frumpy, matronly, slutty, and anything else she can think of, to cover all bases. The correct and only safe response is, "No, honey. You look fantastic. It is both classy and sexy at the same time. But it's not the dress that's sexy—it's YOU that makes that dress look sexy!" Fellas, trust me on this one. This keeps you out of the doghouse, and you'll thank me for it later.

When it's time to go to the event, she'll be on cloud nine, feeling like a million bucks and projecting that feeling to everyone. Guests will tell her how beautiful she looks, and she'll have a great time and love you more for helping her "decide" on the right dress. Here's the clincher: The only place you'll ever see that dress again is hanging in the closet. She'll never wear it again. She can't! "People" have seen her in it! Oh my! Is this weird or is it just me? C'est la vie. We don't have to understand women to love them, do we?

A woman can also usually tell you what every other woman at an event was wearing after you've left. They've noticed it all. They can also retain that information to compare those outfits to what the same women are wearing at an event eight months later, down to the earrings. Guys, I know I must be boring you to death, but what you absolutely need to take away from this is to remember it when you're dressing yourself for business functions, networking, and other social events.

Am I telling you to buy dozens of ties, suits, shirts, and shoes so you never wear the same thing twice? No. Just be aware. The women you do business with are keenly observant of what you're wearing, all the time. They even remember your own wardrobe better than you do. Do you remember the suit and tie you wore to the last event you went to? Of course you don't. But all the women at that event probably do. Just keep that in mind.

Another way that women judge men is by what that 2 percent out there are doing. They are trying to get ready for it, as illustrated in our worst-case scenario theory, so they are equipped to deal with bad behavior, should the time come.

You and I don't even know each other, but the women in my circle are judging me based on what you are doing and vice versa. We are a man team and we need to wise up and help and support one another. This means that we're always representing our gender and creating an image of what can be expected of us.

If you think I'm exaggerating, think about all the famous men out there who have their dirty laundry aired in public: scandalous affairs, secretive bigamy, physical abuse, cheating and stealing from employers, being overprotective and possessive of women as if they're property, and even drunken bar brawls. Have you ever felt the repercussions of this while you're just going about your business, having committed none of these acts? Have you noticed that people sometimes tend to view others differently, or more suspiciously, after these stories are broadcast in the news?

A few years ago a well-known politician was found guilty of having an affair, not just with one woman, but with two—at the same time. Yes, I'm talking about a ménage-a-big trouble. Of course, both women happened to be drop-dead gorgeous, which got my own very beautiful wife's mind racing even more. As we lay stretched on the bed, relaxing, watching this scandal unfold on the news, she turns to me and asks (I'm pretty sure you know what's coming), "Honey? You wouldn't ever have an affair, would you?" That question seems fair to me and it wouldn't, have made me nervous because I honestly wouldn't and almost more importantly, I had my answer ready. I was all primed with my answer: "Of course not, honey. You're all I ever need."

But that's not what she asked. What she wanted to know was, "Honey, you wouldn't ever want to be with two women at once like that, would you?" Gulp. What I'd want and what I'd actually do are two very different things for me, being a reasonable married guy, dedicated to his wife, but after all, still very testosterone inspired. I sure wouldn't do it, but asking if I wanted to do it made me feel guilty and I hadn't even done anything! I answered emphatically, "No, honey. You are all I will ever need"; perhaps after pausing for one second longer than I should have, just for the shock of the question. Would I want to be with two leggy, gorgeous, insatiable nymphomaniacs at the same time? I was still thinking about that when she playfully smacked me saying, "You lie! Of course you would! Every man wants that. Look how successful that guy is and he did it. So you probably want the same. Men!"

All of us are being assessed, judged, categorized, stereotyped, and generalized from the moment we step out of our homes to when we go to bed at night (and as you've seen, it sometimes doesn't stop there). This is life. What the few do, the many pay for.

It was the last part of this accusation that annoyed me. I wouldn't cheat, but simply had male thoughts and desires. Because of this I was now in the same category as this crass, not-too-smart politician. I was guilty by association. This is the quintessential example of how the exception becomes the perception.

We men must individually perform better to help the Man Team. Think about taking one for the team the next time you feel the urge to do something that even feels a little bit like something you might get into trouble for. Let's keep in mind that our individual conduct around women affects the whole of us, and let "Take one for the team" be our new mantra with enhanced meaning.

♀ She Says . . .
The Best Place to Pick Up Women

One afternoon I was having a beer with some male buddies and the conversation meandered around to that old favorite topic: where to meet people that you'd like to date. They all agreed on preferences for pickup hot spots like networking events and gyms. I was at the same time both fascinated and appalled by this. When I probed deeper, their reasoning included a perfect explanation for why this cycle of inappropriate dressing and lecherous behavior keeps chasing its tail round and round.

The guys recounted many networking events at which they witnessed around two of every 50 women dressed as if they'd been getting ready to go out clubbing and accidentally wound up here instead. All men at the event are visibly distracted by this, some gawking and others sneaking glances discreetly. Every man is watching, and most are pretending they are not. The remaining 48 women in the room, though dressed appropriately for the event, are not getting the attention they came to the event for— business.

Ironically, the two racy dressers will complain about the men staring at them, not taking them seriously, and hitting on them. Yes, these are often the same women who post revealing photos of themselves on their social networking sites, creating sexy profiles, not business profiles. Yes, they are social networking after all, but there are a couple of reasons this doesn't help women. A lot of people mix business and pleasure and inevitably have a large draw of both professional and personal "friends" on sites like Facebook. I'm used to seeing women make the mistake of posting their cleavage-revealing photos in mixed company on Facebook, but now those inappropriate photos are showing up on LinkedIn, a site used solely for business networking. Ugh!

These same women want me to recommend them for jobs when they are out there showcasing their "assets," much to my discomfort. Though they may be perfectly qualified for the job in question, those photos damage their credibility, so I'm backed into a corner.

My co-authors are very uneasy about this. If they connect with this kind of profile in any way, the next thing that happens is a guilty-by-association problem. Sometimes business connections are made via LinkedIn or Facebook that seem pretty smart. Then the person changes their photo to something less than savory or writes something a little too racy in your blog's discussion forum, and you've got a problem like this: Someone may be perusing Ivan's or Frank's profile and see that they are connected with Ms. Lowcut-Leopard-Sweater-Hot-Pink-Lipstick and bam! They appear as lacking in judgment as she does, thereby putting their whole reputation into question.

This is exactly why my male friends think picking up women at networking events is effective. All three of us worry about the message it sends when we are linked to cleavage-revealing connections.

Are People Confused About the Purpose of Networking Events?

If I sent out invitations for my 5-year-old son's birthday, detailed with information promising a clown, games, and goodie bags, wouldn't it be clear exactly what kind of event you would be attending? Imagine if my sister were to bring her socially inept boyfriend, Lee (the names have been changed to protect the innocent) to the party, and Lee decides he's going to bring his famous weight-loss products and try to hook in some of the mothers as new customers. He starts setting up a table to show off his merchandise and is attracting stares of disbelief, but then some of the mothers get curious and, though I am in obvious irritation, start asking him about his products. Soon, a gaggle of women are clucking their tongues over what the products promise and getting out their purses, while the children play unsupervised.

How would you feel if this happened? Maybe a little betrayed? If I really did have a wonderfully planned birthday party for my kid and some moron decided to commandeer the event to his advantage, I would view that as a siege, and I'd expect my friends to "do battle with me." I am a very loyal person. My fantasy for this situation would be that my friends would find this unacceptable and say things like "I'm going to tell him that he can't do that. You go tend to the kids. Don't worry, we'll handle this." I'd expect a little sisterhood! Almost every woman I know wants to lose weight, but there wouldn't even be a question of temptation to slink over and connect with him about his product, because the strength of Team Woman is more important!

I would feel deserted if my friends decided that a little bit of temptation was more important than spending quality time with the kids at the party. Do you see the analogy? If this happened a couple of times, women would expect children's birthday parties to be great places to stock up on fabulous weight loss products. Would anyone be even interested in the kids anymore? We need to keep our eyes focused on the goal—strong, communicative, directed networking. The more personal responsibility we each take on, the less the power the few have to create a reputation for the many.

Some unfortunate comments from our male survey members show how this cycle just gets stronger with every turn:

I don't mean to be a sexist, but the good-looking businesswoman will always draw a larger crowd at a function, and businessmen assume that giving business to this attractive woman somehow makes them more likeable to her.

Dealing with very attractive women may influence your business approaches.

Men tend to be more willing to help an attractive female.

There is a difference between being attractive and dressing for sexual interest. Very attractive women can shut down flirting while remaining pleasant and firmly business oriented.

What Were You Trying to Sell?

Our strongest drive as a species is that for sex. That is why sex works to sell most anything to most of the population. We even used sex to sell this book to you, or at least pique your interest until you found deeper meaning in its pages. But first we had to get you to pick it up and look at it, didn't we? If you want to sell a car, just drape a few scantily clad women over it. If you'd like to sell beer, depict a scene in which a classic nerd has a gaggle of well-endowed models hanging on his arm as he chugs from the bottle.

Half-dressed women have been used to sell things to men for years. There is the insinuation that if the guy buys the product, he'll also get the babes. Even men who are happily married or in monogamous, satisfying relationships have the desire to think of themselves as virile, maybe even to the extent of being the only inseminator of an entire village.

OK, that may seem dramatic, but in both the animal and human kingdoms the blatant proof that males want their own offspring to triumph is evident in many places. The drive to fertilize many females in early evolution is why we are here today. I realize that I'm not telling you anything you don't know, but the strength of this drive is what people forget when they create chaos. Have you ever heard of a crazy maker? Yes, this is a person who does one thing, but acts like they want something else. It makes people around them feel like they're going nuts!

Pick up any men's magazine or just spend an afternoon watching football and count how many products are sold to men by using scantily clad women as bait. The chemicals in men's brains make them vulnerable to this kind of manipulation. Of course, men can control themselves. That's what ethics and discipline are. But why make the road to achieving goals littered with landmines that set us up for failure? Men are visual. They're distracted by breasts even when they're trying hard to concentrate on something else. Period.

In her book, *For Women Only*, Shaunti Feldhahn finds out through conducting hundreds of interviews how visual men really are, concluding that even happily married men are distracted by attractive women.

Where Should I Rest My Eyes? Gazing at the Name Badge

One of the most common tips I find myself repeating for men networking with women is regarding the awkward placement of the nametag upon the chest. My strong advice for men is to look into a woman's eyes and not at her chest. But what should we do about the dreaded nametag conundrum? At least twice during the beginning of a conversation I find myself having to recheck the nametag of the person to whom I'm speaking. No matter that I just read the name "Marsha" on her tag, as the conversation picks up and we drift in and out of several topics, I find myself having to recheck Mindy's (or was it Marla's?) name badge. Oh, yes. Marsha. Now I can call her by her name as I talk to her, something all humans like.

There are three conflicting facts here; we all like to hear the sound of our own names, the badge is on the chest, and men are not supposed to stare at the chest area in a business situation. What's a guy to do? This can make an otherwise calm, confident man confused and nervous if he overthinks it.

As you'd expect, this stirs up the age-old topic of how easily men are distracted by breasts. One gentleman told me he'd find it helpful if women didn't put their name badges on their chests because he is so worried they'll think he's looking at you-know-what. I empathize, but where would be a better place for them, on the forehead?

A male colleague recently told me that he hates lanyards because he's been "taught his whole life NOT to look at that part of a woman!" I noticed that a woman standing near us had her lanyard swinging between her voluptuous cleavage as she walked and recalled another comment made by a frustrated woman in our study: "I find that men are more interested in my ample bosoms than my business. Regardless of the fact that I definitely don't flaunt them, most men 'talk to the both of me'. This lack of focus makes it tough for me to be taken seriously as a competent businesswoman." I saw the plight of both my friend and the women trying to corral focus toward their credentials and skills.

No One Will Take You Seriously in That Get-Up

Ladies, when you're attending a business networking event, dress to get business, not a date. If you want to be taken seriously, stop fooling around

OGLING OR MEMORIZING?
STOP GETTING BUSTED!

Gentlemen, glancing quickly at a name badge is very different from ogling the breasts. We can most of the time tell the difference between a couple of refresher looks at the tag and a lingering, repeated, and invasive stare. Here are a few tips for breaking the cycle of unwanted looking:

- *It's hard to be fully involved in a conversation and leering at body parts at the same time.* If you're really listening and fully engaged in the conversation, it'll curb your ogle tendencies. Try asking questions you don't normally ask to keep your mind focused.

- *The first time you meet someone and look at their nametag, say the name aloud and picture it written across their forehead.* Visualizing something written helps to remember it and it'll keep your eyes in the face zone.

- *Use additional mnemonics.* There are three things that need to occur to commit anything to memory: observation, association, and visualization. For more thorough coaching on memorizing, read the helpful tutorials on www.buildyourmemory.com.

and look the part. What is appropriate? It's possible that some of the confusion lies in our corporate culture. A *USA Today* article interviewed several companies whose definition of business casual varied, but Five Point Capital, a San Diego-based equipment-leasing specialist, asks that no body parts from the shoulders to the knees be seen, except for arms. That makes it pretty clean, doesn't it? Even though they allow jeans on Fridays, they're spelling out what nonsexy is, so there's no confusion. A study conducted by www.theladders.com included 2,243 executives, 36 percent of whom thought casual dressers seemed more creative. But 49 percent felt those casual dressers ran the risk of not being taken seriously. Many companies have taken away the casual Friday approach because it got out of hand. Fifty-three percent of employers offered business casual to its employees, compared to only 38 percent just five years later, according to the *USA Today* study.

Managing Perceptions with Your Professional Wardrobe

Need some tips on the best way to lead with your skills instead of your looks? The idea is to wear something that looks crisp, clean, well-tailored, and classy. Here are some guides for appropriate business dress, complete with photos and instruction:

Women: http://businessnetworkingandsex.com/women-dress/

Men: http://businessnetworkingandsex.com/men-dress/

Consider these suggestions from business etiquette expert, professional speaker, corporate trainer, and author Lydia Ramsey (http://mannersthatsell.com). Lydia's book, *Manners That Sell: Adding the Polish That Builds Profits*, is filled with ways to align your appearance and presence with your business goals.

- *Start with a skirted suit or pantsuit for the most conservative look.* A skirted suit is the most professional. With a few exceptions, dresses do not offer the same credibility unless they are accompanied by matching jackets.
- *Skirts should be knee-length or slightly above or below.* Avoid extremes. A skirt more than two inches above the knee raises eyebrows and questions.
- *Pants should break at the top of the foot or shoe.* While Capri pants and their fashion cousins that come in assorted lengths from midcalf to ankle are the latest trend, they are out of place in the conservative business environment.
- *Blouses and sweaters provide color and variety to woman's clothing, but should be appealing rather than revealing.* Inappropriate necklines and waistlines can give the wrong impression.

- *Women need to wear hose in the business world.* Neutral or flesh-tone stockings are the best choices. Never wear dark hose with light-colored clothing or shoes. Keep an extra pair of stockings in your desk drawer unless the hosiery store is next door or just down the street from the office.

- *Faces, not feet, should be the focal point in business, so choose conservative shoes.* A low heel is more professional than flats or high heels. In spite of current fashion and the sandal rage, open-toed or backless shoes are not office attire. Not only are sandals a safety hazard, they suggest a certain official agenda.

- *When it comes to accessories and jewelry, less is once again more.* Keep it simple: one ring per hand, one earring per ear. Accessories should reflect your personality, not diminish your credibility.

Generally speaking, most women who attend networking events and business functions dress professionally, and I am probably preaching to the choir, but we all have to be aware of how the exception creates the perception. Not all men are staring at body parts, and not all women dress like they're going to a rave, but the few that do get all the attention.

It's kind of like a traffic jam with an accident at the end. No one really wants to be sitting in traffic and almost everyone wonders in an irritated way what the holdup is. We crane our necks to see what could possibly be taking so long. When we finally reach the cause of the problem, we too, slow down our cars, adding to the traffic jam, to gawk at the grisly accident. It's not the preferred way to spend an hour on the freeway, and it's not what you came for, but the scene is such a mess that you can't help but stare. To add insult to injury, a lot of the people staring will be thinking to themselves "Now, how the heck did that guy wrap his car around a tree like that?" and the next thing they know they've rear-ended the motorist in front of them because they ceased to remember what they came there to do: get from point A to point B safely.

The one or two who create a distracting scene at an event by being out-of-the-box in a negative way get more attention than the people who do things right. The men wind up thinking women go to networking events to get dates, meet men, or have a good time. This is not the kind of perception we want, because it leads to this:

I find that I get hit on at networking events more than I get approached for business reasons. It's definitely a pattern.

SALE, REFERRAL, OR BOTH?

Not only will that tight little shirt and spiked heels not help your credibility, but it also won't glean referrals. Remember this quote by an anonymous, trusted business authority for guidance while dressing:

"Sex sells, but it does not refer."

We don't have to all dress like nuns or softer versions of men, but we do have to dress in a manner such that if someone were to see us on the street, they could guess by our attire alone that we were about to attend a business-related function. There should be no guessing about that. Now let's dig into the survey results in greater detail.

2

Men and Women, So Much in Common,

But Such Different

Perspectives and Motivators

The Survey Says . . .

Has Networking Played a Role
in Your Success?

One of the first questions we asked the respondents was whether networking was an integral part of their success. More than 91 percent said "yes" (see Figure 2.1 on page 26). Ninety-one percent is practically a tidal wave of agreement. When was the last time you remember 91 percent of businesspeople agreeing on anything? The united front they created by agreeing so heartily on this one question was overwhelming, and a critical impetus for the creation of this book. Networking is critical to the success of businesspeople all over the world.

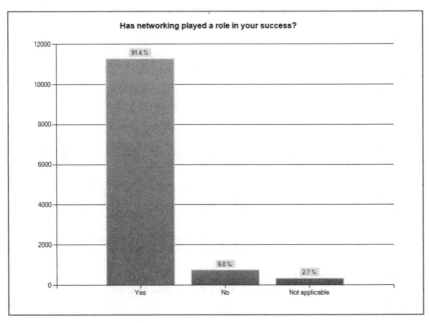

FIGURE 2.1—**Has Networking Played a Role in Your Success?**

A few months ago, I had lunch with the president of a Southern California university and the dean of its affiliated business school. We spoke of many things, but the president specifically asked for my recommendation for ways the business school could better teach its students. I didn't even have to think about it. I told him to start teaching classes on networking, social capital, and emotional intelligence.

We give people bachelor's degrees in marketing, business, and even entrepreneurship, but we teach them hardly anything about the one subject that virtually every businessperson says is critically important—networking.

When he asked me why, I told him that the most thriving entrepreneurs credit their gains to networking, referrals, and investments in building personal relationships. Additionally, the key factors to successful networking interactions are social capital and emotional intelligence. In other words, successful businesspeople are dedicated to building personal relationships, have keen emotional intelligence skills (or develop them), and networking perseverance.

Wealth Beyond Measure

What exactly is emotional intelligence? You may have heard that term loosely thrown around a lot lately as researchers are speedily discovering its importance, even beyond IQ, to predict a person's success in life. Emotional intelligence is the ability to identify, read, assess, and control one's own emotions, as well as a keen awareness of the emotions of others. A high emotional intelligence quotient gives the ultimate power of connection and improves communication in all facets of life.

IQ, EQ, AND SOCIAL CAPITAL

People may get hired because of their intelligence quotient (IQ), but they get promoted because of their emotional quotient (EQ). Social capital is resources that are developed through personal and professional relationships.

The wealth of discovery unearthed every day about emotional quotient and social capital is astounding. Great strides are being made as sociologists, psychologists, and scientists find links tying personal and professional success, and even physical health, to highly developed EQs and well-developed social capital.

I told the dean how important these facets are to completing a solid business education and asked why they aren't being offered in the curriculums of business schools everywhere. Both the president and the dean looked at one another and then the dean replied haughtily, "My professors would never teach that material here. It's all soft science."

Excuse me? We send budding business students out into the tooth-and-nail world of business without what virtually every entrepreneur says is one of the most important elements of success? We give bachelor's degrees in marketing, business, and even entrepreneurship with hardly a crumb of social science or networking practice to prepare them for the biggest bridge to building a network of confident referrals and repeat customers? Teaching people how to interact effectively is soft science?

"What about leadership?" I asked the dean. "You teach leadership, don't you? How are courses in leadership less of a soft science than networking?" He had no answer.

Networking is a field that is finally being codified and structured. This "soft science," along with social capital and EQ, is being taught, though unfortunately not in our major business schools. Much like advanced sales training, networking can be found only in post-degree

THE FUTURE OF BUSINESS EDUCATION

Despite the benefits of social media, face-to-face networking is still the most effective and powerful way to achieve your goals and to help others. It still isn't taught enough in college.

I believe that as more and more business schools open their doors to professors who want to include networking in their marketing curriculum, we will see a major shift in the landscape. We'll see business schools actually teaching a subject that businesspeople say is important. We'll see entrepreneurs coming out of universities equipped with another strategy for business success. We'll see networking utilized at optimum capacity in the business world.

—Wayne Baker, Ph.D., Robert P. Thome Professor of Business Administration, and Professor of Management and Organizations for the Stephen M. Ross School of Business at the University of Michigan (http://waynebaker.org)

programs such as those of entrepreneur Brian Tracy and professional organizations such as BNI and The Referral Institute.

Networking is the mechanism for developing word-of-mouth techniques and social capital together, each highly crucial components of creating business. Business schools around the world need to get serious about teaching this vital element of success. In much the same way businesses that fail to adopt cutting-edge technologies will fall to the wayside, so too will schools that neglect to include these courses. Educators with actual business experience know this and must feel frustration, acknowledging the gap between the real and simulated worlds of education and actual life.

Many of the seasoned professionals who took part in our study emphasized the importance of networking skills as an integral part of understanding business. This respondent even felt its power as a way to equalize opportunities:

Networking creates a level playing field for men and women, equalizing us and enabling us to learn from one another's experiences, both good and bad. I highly recommend networking to anyone who wants to learn, grow, and be highly successful in life's journey. This is definitely the environment in which you can achieve your goals.

Another respondent went one step further, adding a point that many studies have substantiated:

Most business opportunities are either found or created by networking.

These quotes express just how life-changing networking really is:

It is interesting to trace pivotal moments (business AND personal) back in time and discover that they typically originated from a very tiny decision—usually a choice to talk or meet with someone, or to reach out. Knowing that, I always value each new contact as a possible life-changing moment (for both sides).

Earlier in my career, I belonged to an executive women's service club. During the course of that membership, I was fired from a very good job.

I went to the next club meeting with my tail between my legs, stood up to introduce myself as we always did for each other, and told them about my day. By the end of the meeting, those women had three appointments for me for new jobs! It was wonderful.

Almost every job I've gotten over the course of my career is a result of networking. In each case a friend or business associate referred me.

As more business schools hire professors who want to include networking in their marketing curriculum, we will see a major shift in the landscape. Business schools will actually be honoring what professionals say is important, and entrepreneurs will emerge from universities more skilled and prepared for success strategies. Only then will networking be utilized at optimum capacity in the world of industry.

Now let's look at the survey results to understand the way networking wields such power.

The Role Networking Plays in Success, By Gender

As you can see in Figure 2.2, both women and men overwhelmingly agreed that networking played a role in their success. More women than men answered positively, and though the difference is small, it is statistically significant.

Some respondents, such as this one, thought that women were actually better at networking than men:

Women are better networkers than men. They take longer to trust people, but if you use nonthreatening approaches and utilize follow-up, you will succeed with them.

Additional differences become even more apparent when the data was flipped to compare the yes and no responses. Notice in Figure 2.3 on page 31 that men, by a fairly wide margin, made up a much larger percentage of the group who felt networking did not play a role in their success. You will see that those people who said "no" tended to be men

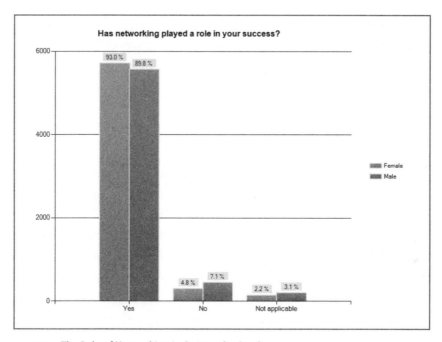

FIGURE 2.2—**The Role of Networking in Success, by Gender**

What is your gender?			
Has networking played a role in your success?			
	Yes	**No**	**Response Totals**
Female	**50.7%**	40.1%	**50.0%**
	(5,709)	(294)	**(6,003)**
Male	49.3%	**59.9%**	50.0%
	(5,561)	**(440)**	(6,001)
Answered question	11,270	734	**12,004**
Skipped question			0

FIGURE 2.3—**Opinions on Attributing Networking to Success, By Gender**

WHAT DOES "STATISTICALLY SIGNIFICANT" REALLY MEAN?

"**S**tatistically significant" is a term that sometimes confuses people, but it really means that the results are solid and if the same study were to be conducted 100 more times, 95 of them (or more) would yield the same results.

Imagine that you're running a marathon and all the conditions are perfect on the day the race is held. The weather is a comfortable 60 degrees Fahrenheit, you've got your most comfortable shorts and T-shirt on, and you're feeling fit and well prepared. There's only one tiny thing that doesn't fall into the perfect category. It's something you notice at mile five: a minuscule pebble in your shoe. Even though it is so small that you could barely see it if you had the time to take your shoe off, the blister it creates could make or break your running time. A pebble in a runner's shoe is statistically significant, though very small.

As you can understand from that analogy, "statistically significant" also means that the tiny result is something that cannot be ignored, and usually either indicates or causes other things.

by a fairly wide margin, almost 60 percent. Only 40 percent who felt networking wasn't part of their success were women. Consequently, while most people said that networking played a role in their success, slightly more were women.

Why did more women than men feel that networking played a role in their success? Some of the comments by the survey respondents shed light on the answer as shown here:

I believe that my success with networking and receiving referrals comes because of my inherent nature to nurture. The nurturing aspect is what drives me to see a project through to the end, to make sure my client is successful. This same drive makes me a good networker, but not a pushy one. The nurturing instinct may be the biggest difference between men and women networkers.

Whether women are actually more "nurturing" than men in general is beyond our scope here, but these respondents touch on important points:

Women look out for one another and take the time to find out about people.

Women mirror some of their lifelong practiced, childhood-acquired playground social tactics at networking meetings. They seek common ground with others and ask questions that show concern, such as whether or not it was difficult to find parking.

Could the same be said of men? Do early social experiences in the sandbox shape each gender's behavior, values, and perspectives in fundamental ways that impact their adult networking agendas? The woman who shared the comment above certainly thinks so.

Both our data and respondents' comments reveal that women place a premium on the relational aspects of networking and emphasize the importance of spending time getting to know fellow network members. Here's an example of one:

The circle of women I network with feels truly supportive. I became a member in 1999 and have since grown professionally, as have the other members. I lost my mother and sister since becoming a member. Knowing that these women knew what I was going through and that it was an inspiration for them to see how I handled work during that, was the best feeling. I have never experienced anything like that with men.

Again, we see a female respondent crediting the nurturing by fellow women as an important component of her networking experience—also conspicuously noting that the men she's been exposed to differ in that regard.

♂ He Says . . .

The first thing we've got to define is the way success for men and women is different. Understanding what is important to each gender will help us understand why they use the criteria they do to deem themselves successful (or not). This understanding isn't to just give us a sense of comfort and being on the same page—because we're not! We're very different in what motivates us. Understanding what motivates one another affords an inside advantage to both business and personal communication, and ultimately helps us affect the bottom line. Uncovering what both men and women define as success will also show why women rated themselves higher than men.

If you ask a man to define whether or not his networking efforts have been successful, he will come up with an answer based on how many deals he's closed as a result of them. He's got this little abacus in his head and the beads are clicking away, tallying how many conversations came to monetary fruition. When the beads of the abacus total a bottom line that he approves of, that's success to him. He's been motivated by the idea of production and acquisition since his ancient, prehistoric roots.

Back when we were cave dwellers it wasn't much different, really. I can imagine myself in that era, acquiring, providing, bringing home food for my family, feeling satisfied and proud of my accomplishments, which today translates as "closing the deal." My caveman self-esteem would have been high if I managed to keep them wanting for nothing. What I'd bring home would be the bottom line and that would create my definition of how successful I was.

She Comments . . .

I can imagine the satisfied grunting and business-appropriate loincloth for the hunt.

He Responds . . .

OK, loincloths aside, it really can be traced back to our simple beginnings. Just as early man determined some of the traits modern man still carries, imagine the cave diva of days gone by, acquiring a network of cave sisters for the purpose of raising children, gathering resources, and supporting each other communally in those harsh times.

Similarly, if you ask modern woman to rate her networking success, the little abacus in her head will be tallying up all the new relationships she's developed, and if the number is high, she'll consider herself successful. She also may quantify her success by how much she has enriched the quality of current relationships and improved her networking and conversing skills.

What happened to the bottom line? How can there be success with no bottom line? How ridiculously unproductive and silly is that? Business networking is supposed to be for getting results that translate to business. It's not about building friendships and having fun. It's also not supposed to be for just building endless relationships that don't yield anything. It's all about what you can get from each relationship.

What's blatantly obvious by now is that men and women define success differently. We each have our own personal definitions of it based on what we perceive as desirable achievements. For men it's quantified by bigger sales, greater profits, expansion of territory, new market opportunities, products or services we can sell, and strategic alliances that may bring us more business in the future.

I personally would rather have fewer people in my network netting me the lion's share of my profits than dozens of friendly new connections not bringing in any cash! Men, are you with me? Do you agree that plumping up the bottom line is what networking is all about?

Man Team, I'm sorry to have to do this to you. If you agreed with me on that then you're wrong. If that's how you're running your networking agenda, then you're most likely losing quite a lot of business. Moving around comfortably in networking circles and averaging the greatest possible bottom line over time requires that you do a few things differently. First of all, you've got to play by women's rules instead of your own. Women want strong relationships, and if you cater to that, not only will you build your circle of trust with the ladies, but your new relationship skills will also allow you to build more long-term connections with men.

She Comments . . .

When we women build up the foundations of relationships over time with proof of loyalty and quality performance, then we feel that bridge of strength and trust begin to build. That's a relationship! Once the trust begins to grow, we have confidence. When confidence and trust are achieved, loyal and ongoing business-related results follow. Doesn't that seem like a better way to do things, guys? Don't you first want to know who's going to leave you high and dry and who's going make you shine before you put your reputation on the line and bring them into your inner circle?

He Responds . . .

We men don't quite do it that way, do we? If someone I network with isn't connecting me to financial gain in one way or another, then I pretty quickly determine that they aren't an asset to me and don't continue putting effort into the relationship.

Wait a minute. Does this really make sense, guys? Can you really make a determination that quickly on whether or not a relationship is going to turn up something big for you later on? Can you really predict who's going to give you your next high-net-worth referral and when they're going to give it to you?

I am certainly not suggesting that you forget about the "bottom line" or remove it from your definition of success. What I am strongly encouraging is that you expand that definition to include the relationship-building process to yield more business over time.

One more question: Can you remember the last person you decided not to keep in contact with anymore because they just weren't sending any business your way? Are you positive they weren't going to send you a very high-net-worth referral in the future? Let that ring in your mind for a while. Don't beat yourself up, though.

One Man's Journey Through Feminine Networking Realization

Since the beginning of my career I had a sense that getting to know people was important. In the scheme of staying on top of showcasing my business I already also knew back then that the most important ways to market myself were also usually connected to the most productive sales venues. Though I understood the importance of connecting socially to others to increase the bottom line, I didn't call it networking; rather, I just thought of it as getting to know people.

When I learned about the concept of focused, structured networking, I dove in with enthusiasm. I thought that the strategic development of relationships for the purpose of people helping one another excel in business was very cool. In fact, I thought I was pretty good at it.

In the beginning, it seemed to be working. My business grew as did the sales calls, referrals, and closing ratios. I considered myself successful in networking. It wasn't as consistent as I thought it would be, and as time went on it started to lose its effectiveness. Naturally, I saw this as a sign that I needed to increase my group population, so I invited more people to be part of my network. I also stepped up the requests for leads and referrals. Then it slowed down even more, and I was stumped.

As I struggled to understand why my hard work wasn't creating results, I remembered a quote I'd heard years before. "It's not what you're doing that matters as much as the way that you're doing it." Hmmm. I stopped to really ponder the idea of the way I was working. Was I working smart or hard? I realized that it was the latter. I was just putting in a lot of sweat equity, but not understanding the science behind it, or the most effective way to do it. I was just doing what I had always done—working very hard and thinking that that would make things happen.

Then I found out about a referral meeting. Though the idea sparked my interest, my cynical New Yorker gene scoffed, "Yeah. Right. A meeting where people refer business back and forth to one another and it actually works? And I'm Prince Charming." The skeptic in me won and I didn't go to that meeting, nor did I accept the many invitations that followed over the next six months.

For some unknown reason I finally found myself at one of those meetings, and the way it actually worked blew me away. The weekly opportunity within those meetings to refer thousands of dollars of business got me hooked. Those were my first BNI meetings, and they began the learning process that changed how I view business relationships and my education in using networks effectively. I began working smarter instead of just harder and it made all the difference in the world. Working smarter allowed me to focus more keenly on what I really wanted to do and achieve greater results in less time. I remember thinking that I wish I'd started doing it earlier in my career. I was pretty gung-ho about it. I still am.

The reason I told you that story was to stress the importance of keeping up with current and cutting-edge social and business practices. Even though humans have been networking since the dinosaurs were their biggest worry, the world is new every few years and the way we network and communicate with one another changes with it.

She Comments . . .

My mother's question, "were you raised in a cave?" comes to mind. Though this usually referred to using the wrong fork, modern social methods are sort of silently voted in by societies, and if you don't observe them, you don't get dessert. Or business.

He Responds . . .

Yes, we've got to keep ourselves informed and practiced in the latest developments in business communication, or we'll be left behind. Being left behind translates to being out of business. Period.

In professional networking organizations, much like back in our playground days, both genders can learn networking skills from one another, and this makes for richer, more fruitful experiences for everyone.

Calling all men! Listen up. Our definition of success is not what it should be. We need to build long-term relationships knowing that one referral from one person five years down the road could top your financial goal for the whole year. If I didn't give you a referral for five years and then I gave you one that was the largest or in your all-time top three sales, was it worth the wait?

 ## She Says . . .

Ninety-one percent of our global group of professionals said networking played a role in their success. Doesn't that naturally create a need to understand the communication styles of other genders and cultures? The Referral Institute's "Room Full of Referrals" program is targeted toward identifying each participant's behavior style so that we can recognize those styles in an actual meeting, speak the language they best understand, and observe what is important to them. Boiled down, it allows us to network with each person in the unique way they like to be networked with.

The more we study and learn about one another, the more success we'll have networking. The ladies out there have to learn how men like to network, and what makes them feel comfortable and successful. It will help us be taken more seriously by them if they see us doing some of the things that are important to them.

Networking is about interacting with actual, flesh-and-bone humans, and not just by way of the internet, or even the phone. The popularity of social media networking sometimes confuses the importance of the actual and leaves the process incomplete. You can't just sit in front of a computer, making online "friends," or just join an online business network and expect that to create an actual circle of solid referrals you can count on. Nor would you want to follow up on leads to professionals that you don't have the advantage of having physically gotten to know over time through proof of work ethic, would you? How can you vouch for someone and have someone vouch for you if you only know their cyber self?

He Comments . . .

Tell it like it is, sister! I know I tend to be single-minded when it comes to just making sure I get that business, but investing networking time and confidence, then counting on the bottom line, from a virtual connection leaves me feeling a little queasy.

She Responds . . .

It all boils down to each gender really understanding the other, and you can't do that without practice and face-to-face observation.

Ladies, the other half of the population is men, no? So wouldn't it serve us well to learn how to network in their language? It will make us more successful, not to mention make the whole process a lot more fun. Hold onto your purses—it's going to be a wild ride!

Genders Credit Networking Important to Success

Ninety-three percent of women felt networking played a role in their success, while 89.9 percent of men felt the same way. It may not seem a big gap in numbers, but as Ivan "The Survey" Misner defined "statistically significant" for us recently, I'm sure you'll remember the tiny pebble in the marathoner's shoe story and see the reason we keep track of numbers.

Ladies, are any of you shocked that more men than women feel responsible for their own success without the help of others? I'm sure those guys also feel completely responsible for their own births and upbringing, too. Their poor mothers!

This directly relates to how men responded to the question, "How did you learn to network?" More men said they learned it on their own, so it makes sense that higher numbers of these supermen would also not attribute networking to part of their success. Heck, these are the same guys that won't stop and ask for directions with a tank on "E" in the middle of the desert and a woman in labor in the car.

He Comments . . .

Don't you think you might be exaggerating just a little bit?

She Reponds . . .

Maybe. Let's get back to the survey results to help illustrate my point. It's not surprising that more women than men say networking contributes to their success when you think about how collaborative we are by nature. Let's use your cave-dwelling era as an example, Frank, and imagine all the things the cave gals did to form community, such as working in shifts to keep the fires burning while the he-men were out hunting, or sharpening their spears, or something. Imagine those women gathering wood from the forest around them while keeping watch over the clan's children in shifts, or even nursing one another's babies. Women had to form groups and collaborate to survive back in prehistoric days, and that still holds true today, though to less of a survival degree and more of a thriving degree.

The bigger issue under investigation is how success is defined differently by each gender, and why. During one of our writing powwows, co-author Frank and I pored over statistical data that triggered an intricate conversation on that. The fact that women are more relational and men are more business driven seems to directly shape their definitions of success as well as personal identities and self-esteem levels, depending on how well they excel in those areas. That subject matter would be worth an entire survey in itself.

Consider the information below from Dr. Jeff Cornwall, co-founder, president, and CEO of Atlantic Behavioral Health Systems, and author of six books on entrepreneurship:

> *Over the past couple of decades we have seen a steady increase in the number of women becoming entrepreneurs. While the number of women choosing an entrepreneurial career path is approaching that of their male counterparts, the factors that motivate or drive female entrepreneurs are often quite different.*

Many female entrepreneurs—and, in fact, a growing number of young male entrepreneurs—deliberately limit the growth of their businesses to allow themselves time to pursue interests beyond the office. They want to spend time with their family, church, or in their community, or pursue other personal interests such as hobbies or travel.

Erin Albert, author of *Single. Women. Entrepreneurs.*, has this to add: "Women, especially Generations X and Y, want to make their business and personal lives and aspirations work more in harmony. Because of this, they choose to limit the size of their businesses and not pursue outside funding from investors or loans to fuel more growth."

It is my experience from years of coaching women and men that the definition of what is important is the major cause of friction, not to mention all-out roadblocks, in networking between genders. I also believe it is responsible for the reason women feel that they are not taken seriously by the men they network with. Respondents reflect on these experiences here:

Men do not always display respect for women in networking situations.

When a woman stands up to say that she sells skin care and color cosmetics, or that she offers in-home designer clothing shopping so you can comfortably acquire purchases in your living room with friends rather than fighting the crowds at the mall, there are often groans, snickers, or mumbled comments from men in the room. Whether they are simply joking to each other about not wanting to give their wives another reason to spend hard-earned money or downgrading the profession of the woman speaking is not clear. It does, however, come across as a disrespectful, nonsupportive environment, whether or not it's the men's intention.

The men in my network read what Erin Albert and Jeff Cornwell had to say and further justified not taking women seriously with these additional assumptions:

- They must not be the primary breadwinner for the family;
- The don't take their business seriously;
- It is only a part-time hobby, not a businesses;
- They must have other sources of income.

Automatically the men wrote off those women, assuming they were not serious about their businesses. Contrary to the casual-seeming style of a social business like the home shopping party, these companies can and do really thrive. One such example is Denise Praul of Accurate Tax Management (http://accuratetaxmgmt.com). Hers is considered a lifestyle business, which she takes very seriously. Because she is a single woman who can do what she wishes, she shapes the business to conform to her life. It is her primary business and she does quite well. Further kudos to her; she is the only professional in her state with her credentials, having earned rights for certifications that normally only government employees get. She applied for years for this opportunity and was finally awarded the privilege to take the classes last year.

Guys, What Seems to Be the Problem?

Men just create problems for themselves when they fail to recognize and respect other business professionals. The narrow-minded perception of only applauding a business that has the same goals as one's own is unfortunate. Because some of these businesses revolve around a different business model (social or in-home selling), and utilize more of the word-of-mouth and chitchat skills to create a sales presentation, men do not recognize them as important because those aren't the skills they value. Too bad they can't see that at the end of the "gathering" phase, there are acquisition, production, and cold-hard-cash benefits to be gained.

Mary Kay Cosmetics is a perfect example of a business that men tend to not take seriously or recognize as worthy. Though the business is privately owned and does not release financial information, some stats are available on Wikipedia based on income reports from its many global contractors. Founded in 1963 and 1.8 million strong in its global sales force, Mary Kay is speculated to have pulled in $2.5 billion in 2010.

I observe some surprising behavior from men when there is a Mary Kay representative at one of our networking meetings. I watch in dismay as the representative talks about her business and is met with total disregard. Men will neglect to listen while she talks, talking over her in their own conversations, making little jokes and snide remarks, and snickering. Maybe they should look at the sales figures, or consider that a company so successful might be able to give them some pretty decent referrals. Men, you do this silly stuff at your own risk. You're only hurting yourselves.

Mary Kay, the Architect, and the Landscaper

Sounds like a fairy tale, doesn't it? What do an architect, a commercial landscaper, and a Mary Kay rep have in common? A network! One particular Indianapolis BNI chapter has many types of professionals, including these three.

One afternoon, a Mary Kay rep, Laurie Colby, heard from a friend how unhappy he was with the construction of his restaurant. There were all kinds of issues that needed to be resolved. She let him know that she had a network of people she thought might be able to help him. Laurie introduced one of her associates, Paul Ewer of Quantum Architecture, to the restaurateur. Paul got the job to redo the restaurant. He then passed the referral along to another member in the network who wound up redoing all the restaurant's landscaping. Several other members of the network were also hired to help out on this project.

While this story is a great testimony to the importance of not underestimating a woman's business, there's more to it. From that connection, Paul landed a contract to build a series of restaurants across the United States. That connection wound up being one of the most financially valuable contracts in the history of Paul's company.

Paul said that he had never considered the possibility of getting such a heavyweight referral from someone who sells cosmetics, but now will never underestimate a woman's network, no matter what she does for a living!

Conversely, there's another group I've observed with only two women in it, and when I asked the men why it was so male-dominated, they explained, "We just can't find women who take their businesses seriously." It's possible that those men are part of that negative cycle of misunderstanding and that their perception of most of the female entrepreneurs they've met is skewed, so they don't see the potential for including them in the circle, thus limiting their own earning abilities.

Maybe the definition of success in networking is different for each of us, but, if we are going to be more successful, we have to approach each other with open minds and a desire to learn and accept different values. Leading with a desire for understanding can build stronger relationships with our fellow network members, male and female.

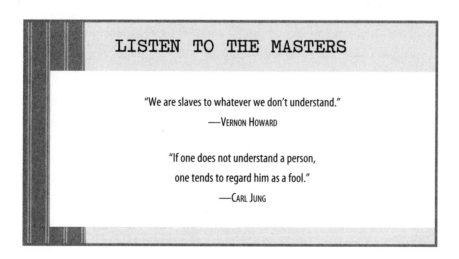

LISTEN TO THE MASTERS

"We are slaves to whatever we don't understand."
—Vernon Howard

"If one does not understand a person,
one tends to regard him as a fool."
—Carl Jung

The Survey Says . . .
Networking Skills

We thought that it would be interesting to see if men and women learned how to network differently. We then asked participants about the different ways they learned. Many of them said all they needed to learn came from just interacting in networking groups. These organizations often have their own training programs and materials, so this is not surprising. It also supports the old wisdom of learning by doing, or learning on the job. People learn fastest by watching other people, making mistakes, and correcting them. Hands-on learning goes that much faster when they are learning a skill that involves interacting.

Most of the respondents chose more than one method of training. Almost half cited just working on their own as a training tool, but many of these people also may have combined that with participation in networking groups or the reading of books and articles as tools, too. More than one-fourth had been mentored, which is widely considered one of the most effective ways to learn anything.

Many women in the survey mentioned mentoring as a way to learn about networking. Here is just one example:

It's nice to mentor and network with other people. Women and men have unique business strengths and I would not know my business as well as I do were I not mentored by both.

According to the survey, women learn networking with more structured methodologies than men do. The differences weren't huge but certainly statistically significant. What is most interesting is that the aids or tools women used greatly varied, but they all dominated the alternative (working alone). In other words, it seems the biggest thing women had in common is that they didn't work alone, and the methods they chose instead spanned the range of the many tools available to them.

Women are more likely to learn by reading books or articles, taking seminars or classes, being mentored, or participating in networking groups. Conversely, the only learning method that men used more than

How have you developed your networking skills? (You may select more than one answer.)					
	Reading books or articles	Taking seminars or classes	Being mentored by someone	Working on my own	Participating in networking group(s)	Response Totals
Female	**52.4%** **(2,786)**	**54.7%** **(2,452)**	**54.2%** **(1,541)**	46.1% (2,510)	**52.4%** **(4,577)**	**50.1%** **(5,562)**
Male	47.6% (2,529)	45.3% (2,027)	45.8% (1,301)	**53.9%** **(2,929)**	47.6% (4,153)	49.4% (5,539)
Answered question	5,313	4,479	2,842	5,439	8,729	**11,101**
Skipped question						2

FIGURE 2.4—**How Men and Women Develop Networking Skills**

women was—wait for it . . . wait for it . . . "working on their own." What a surprise!

One woman from the survey said:

A lot of people tell me the best networker they know is their own mother. I'd agree with that. My own mother is a brilliant networker. I have never met anyone who has told me their father is the best networker they know. Why is this?

Well, ma'am, I'm afraid the answer to your question may be that women appear to do more homework than men! Based on this comprehensive survey, it seems that men just wing it a lot more than women do.

In sum, although both men and women substantially feel that networking played a role in their success, it seemed to be a slightly bigger factor for women than for men. There was a fair amount of agreement between the two on networking learning methods, but women were much more inclined to take advantage of structured learning opportunities than men, as opposed to learning on their own.

♂ He Says . . .

Women read more, take more seminars, more often use the tutelage of mentors, and participate in networking groups more than men. Men, I hope you are embarrassed by this! This is sad. Why was the only area we excelled in that of working on our own? I think I am actually embarrassed to be a man at this moment. Part of the reason is not just because we do less than women to better ourselves, but also that we are willing to admit to it publicly, with no shame, and even a smidge of ignorant pride, no less. (Guys, you could have at least lied in the survey!)

This reminds me of people who actually brag about getting by only using 10 percent of their brains, when untapped human capacity is an estimated 90 percent. You've never heard a woman say that, have you? Nope. Just men. Being stupid is one thing. Admitting to it without shame or intent to improve is another. Bragging about it is just plain stupid!

She Comments . . .

Hey, don't be so hard on yourself. I always knew you'd figure it out. Eventually. I'll be here waiting with fresh, hot coffee when you wake up.

He Responds . . .

Thanks, Hazel!

Guys, are we really so stubborn that we are not willing to commit our time, money, and energy into ongoing learning? Why? Why do we feel we don't need these tools? This makes no sense. Think about all the other tools through history we've recognized a need for, developed, and used to our gain.

Back to my old caveman analogies. I'm reminded of the popular belief that early humans invented the wheel by sliding down a hill on gravel. When they noticed how much more quickly they traveled on wheels (even if they fell on their faces the first few times), an idea was born. That less evolved brain was able to see an advantage and make use of it. Almost more important, now that the wheel (car) has been invented and is being used en masse, there are very few people who just stick to the tools they were already using (legs) and walk 20 miles to work. When tools are available to help you get ahead, use them!

BLAME IT ON BIOLOGY?

The desire to look cool and self-sufficient is a mysterious one. We're not sure if its roots are primitive or ego-related. John Gray, Ph.D. and author of the famous *Men Are From Mars and Women Are From Venus*, sheds some light on the subject:

> There is actually a biological reinforcement that occurs, a feedback loop, that rewards men internally for doing things on their own. When I am able to accomplish something by myself without depending on others, testosterone is released which lowers my stress level. If I have to depend on others, testosterone levels begin to drop and estrogen levels increase, which also goes along with increasing stress levels for men.
>
> It was shown that when men are in competitive activities, their stress levels go down. When they are in cooperative activities and dependent on others, as in harmonious relationships, their stress levels actually go up. These are some of the physiological examples to support what you see even in little children. Little boys want to do things more independently, more on their own. They want to prove that they did something alone because when you do something on your own, it tends to be a testosterone-stimulating activity, whereas, when you do something together it tends to be estrogen stimulating and oxytocin stimulating. Oxytocin is a hormone that has been proven to lower stress levels in women.

She Comments . . .

I wonder if primitive humans first looked around to see who was watching when they fell and hurt themselves the way we modern folk do. It's unbelievable how people can trip and hurt themselves badly, but be primarily concerned with the embarrassment level that follows once they look up and meet the eyes of passersby. Both genders share this silliness!

He Responds . . .

Yes, but men certainly embody it to a greater degree as is evident in knuckle-dragging moves such as drag racing at stoplights, driving very expensive red sports cars to compensate for any number of self-doubts, and the insistence of doing things like rewiring a basement by oneself, even though one is not a qualified electrician, to the point of electric shocks. The reality is that we men want to impress our women folk.

By looking for help, we are admitting to weakness and ignorance. Oh, get over yourself! Do you know what weakness actually is? It's the belief that you know it all, or worse yet, the desire to have people think you do. Strength is admitting to weakness and imperfection and being able to be vulnerable and learn. Here lies the real challenge, should you decide to take it.

Let's talk about the way men build friendships. They do this by doing stuff together. Not sitting around and talking, but actually doing some type of activity. Imagine you are a teenage cave boy and your father, uncle, or other male elder has just passed down the tradition of hunting for food for your family. This mentor would bring you out and teach you the ropes. There's no shame in needing to be taught something new, right? But what if you came from a farming culture instead and were asked to go hunting with male friends. You wouldn't know how, would you? Would it be hard for you to admit that you didn't know how to hunt? After all, in this culture, manhood is based on the ability to provide.

Fast forward to today. You, as the family provider, have to bring in more business. You go to your first networking event. It is important that people see you as successful, smart, and capable, so when you attend the event you don't ask for help. You figure you'll learn as you go. The problem with this is that your success may happen, but slowly and probably not very potently. If you really want to be "the man" of your family, then use bravery and courage to ask for help. The more quickly you learn how to be an effective networker, the faster you'll achieve results for your family. That's the bottom line!

GOOD FACTS FOR MEN TO KNOW

Consider this recent poll, courtesy of the Catalyst 2010 Census (www.catalyst.org), a research organization focusing on women in business:

Percentage of women in the U.S. labor force:	46.3%
Percentage of female Fortune 500 corporate officers:	15.4%
Percentage of female Fortune 500 top earners:	6.7%
Percentage of female Fortune 500 CEOs:	2.4%
Number of female CEOs in Fortune 500 companies:	12
Number of female CEOs in Fortune 501–1000 companies:	10
Total female CEOs in Fortune 1000 companies:	22
Women-owned U.S. employer firms:	910,761
Women employed:	7.6 million
Female payroll earned:	$217.6 billion

Do you feel intimidated yet, men? If we want to continue to compete and thrive, we have to invest in relationships. This means we have to learn how women think. It may not be easy, but it is our mission. Consider this thought from one of our respondents:

I am one of only four men in a women-focused business group of about 100 members. I've found that because I am one of the few men, when I speak, the others will pay extra attention to what I say. But this only works if I keep my comments and thoughts to a minimum. If I start to dominate the conversation, the tone or attitude changes fairly quickly.

Being associated with a women's business group can be very effective, but only if you're willing to take a nondominant approach and are comfortable letting the women completely control the environment.

Some of you men may be thinking that you already know how to get along and work well with women. Really? Do you think so? When women have a choice to hire or professionally partner with a man or a woman, all other things being equal, they'll usually choose a woman; unless there is a strategic reason not to. They do this not just because of her gender, rather, because they feel more of a connection with female counterparts because of their shared relationship-building skills. It's probably being done subconsciously, but, rest assured, it is a strong tendency that we have all seen happen a lot.

It may sound like I'm saying we can't compete with women because we don't have the right equipment, mindset, or cultural insight into life as a woman. That's not what I'm saying at all. If that were true, then this book would be pointless, and it's just the opposite. This book is a tool to give you the advantage of understanding so that you absolutely can compete.

Most women don't have a problem doing business with men, unless the guy in question is just a great big jerk. Normally they don't choose men as their business counterparts because they don't share that communication connection the way they do with other women. This can be overcome. We just need to learn to master the subject matter, the way we'd do with any other challenge.

What about women learning to communicate and work better with men? Isn't that important? After all, we men are still the rulers of the world, aren't we? (Please don't tell my wife I said that, nor any of my female employees.) Of course, this is just as important. Women need to understand the male mindset beyond the hackneyed sports, beer, sex, and toys stereotype. I know a lot of you women reading this just wondered if there really is more to men than sports, beer, sex, and toys. Contrary to popular belief, we are a little more complex than that, and actually pretty intelligent. OK, not always, but at least about stuff that doesn't have to do with sports, beer, sex, and toys.

Stay tuned to look at the male and female psyche and self-perceptions and how they factor into business relationships and transactions.

How Else Are We Different?

In friendship, men bond by doing, not talking. When men get together their purpose is to hunt, fish, work around the house, build, run, bike, swim, play poker, bowl, or anything else that is not talking about stuff. This process of growing friendships through being in motion together begins in early childhood. In elementary school, boys played army, tag, monsters, and superheroes. During the process of playing, boys find out more about one another. They have a review process for deciding if this guy is going to be a pal. Did he cheat? Was he mean, selfish, or a jerk? Did we laugh a lot? Was he open to my ideas? Was it fun? The natural process of play allows us to get to know the potential friend better. Boys don't play with a purpose. It's just fun, but along the way, play reveals whether or not we like the playmate, and how much.

As adult males we do the same. "Doing" together allows us to bond and have meaningful conversations about the stuff we are doing, without the emotional part of talking about feelings. We get to cut out all the drama and as a result, rarely argue or judge each other. We, as men, don't need to judge. If we don't think you're the type of friend we want, we just stop getting together.

She Comments . . .

Is this why some guys say they'll call and never do?

He Responds . . .

You've got it! Keep it simple. That's our creed. We tend to compartmentalize things and don't like to carry a lot of emotional baggage. We want to resolve a problem quickly, when it occurs, and then move on. We get upset, let off steam, and then decide what we are going to do about it.

Then we simply do it or let it go. We don't talk about it for the next two months wondering what to do or rehash it. We let it go and move on.

Why does all this matter? Because women don't operate this way. Their friendships are not about doing but about talking, sharing, helping, thinking, and anything relational. What this means for men and women both is that we need to be aware, learn about, have an understanding for, and be willing to adapt to the opposite sex's expectations and processes of relationship building.

Have you ever met someone and thought about having a romantic relationship with them based on the usual criteria: You liked them, they liked you, you laughed together and got along well? They were funny, witty, smart, caring, thoughtful, compassionate, and very attractive. That was just about everything you wanted. Then you got into a conversation about goals in life. Your desires for kids, career, professional lifestyle, and other important directional goals were polar opposites. You probably felt then that your basic needs were not being met and this was a different person than you had assumed. Then you realized that this may not be the person for you and felt upset, frustrated, angry, and depressed. Part of the problem was that you didn't fully understand this person in the beginning.

This is the same thing we are talking about in a business relationship. This can and does happen between two men and two women, however, it's much more pronounced between the sexes. We have plenty of data that supports what we all already know: Men and women are different. Not vastly different, but significantly different. This means that we are very similar to each other. We have many commonalities. But the differences are very different. Two perfect examples are our sexual organs and brain functions. This book is our attempt to enhance understanding for the ultimate goal of creating a more harmonious and productive work life.

The Difference Is in Our Brains

Here are some interesting differences between men's and women's brains:

RELATIONSHIP BUILDING

Women are much more effective communicators in the relationship-building process than men. Why? They listen more intently and actually hear, focusing on discussion details so any solution that is achieved is a consensus of the group, rather than just a sole opinion from an individual. This allows them to build trust more easily and therefore bond more quickly and deeply. Their natural ability to read and process nonverbal cues such as tone, emotion, and empathy is great.

You men right now are probably thinking that you already do that! Yeah, right. And I used to like to watch *Oprah*!

We men are not natural listeners and discussers. We are problem solvers. We are task-oriented and tend to be more isolated in our processes. These differences explain why men and women sometimes have difficulty communicating and why man-to-man friendships look different from female ones.

LEFT WHEEL VS. DUAL WHEEL DRIVE

Women process equally in both sides of the brain. By using "dual-wheel" brain processing women typically solve problems more creatively than men and are more aware of feelings while communicating.

Men tend to process better in the left hemisphere.

This helps to explain why men are generally stronger in left-brain activities and approach problem-solving from a task-oriented perspective.

MATHEMATICAL ABILITIES

Typically this is not a female strength. The IPL (inferior-parietal lobule) is smaller in women than men. In women, however, it processes sensory information. The larger right side in women allows them to focus on specific stimuli, such as a baby crying in the night.

The IPL brain area is typically significantly larger in men, especially on the left side, than in women. This is the same area that in Einstein's brain was discovered to be abnormally large. This section is thought to control mathematical ability, and supports men being more logical than emotional, because mathematics is a study of logic. How many women do you know that like Spock on Star Trek? I can't think of any. He was way too logical to be liked by women. To men, he made great sense. He was mathematical in his thinking.

STRESSFUL SITUATIONS

Women gather that which is important to them to protect and nurture. Psychologist Shelley E. Taylor coined the phrase "tend and befriend" after recognizing that during times of stress women take care of themselves and their children (tending) and form strong group bonds (befriending).

Here's something interesting: The reason for these different reactions to stress is rooted in hormones. The hormone oxytocin is released during stress in everyone. However, estrogen tends to enhance oxytocin, resulting in calming and nurturing feelings, whereas testosterone, which men produce in high levels during stress, reduces the effects of oxytocin.

Men generally have a "fight or flight" response to stress situations. This means that when we are faced with a stressful situation, we will instinctively either take it head-on or totally avoid and not deal with it. Most men are not very good at the in-between. As the true problem solvers that men are, they want the issue resolved immediately, and if they are not going to do it personally they will the resolve it by not dealing with it. Once they decide they are not dealing with it, they conclude that the problem is resolved. (Dumb, yes, but that is who we are.)

SUPERIOR VERBAL SKILLS

Two sections of the brain responsible for language were found to be larger in women than in men, which supports why women typically excel in language-based subjects and in language-associated thinking. Women process language in both hemispheres.

Men tend to only process language in our dominant hemisphere. Gentlemen, this means that you will rarely, if ever, win an argument with a woman. You just don't have the vocabulary or the marathon speaking ability to make it across the finish line. Just go have a beer and wait until it's over.

EMOTIONAL CONNECTIONS

Women typically have a larger deep limbic system than men, which allows them to be more in touch with their feelings and better able to express them, which promotes bonding. Because of this ability to connect, more women serve as caregivers for children. Could this be why women tend to be better at building such strong networks?

We men are not as in touch with our feelings, or if we are, we are certainly not comfortable using the information we get from observing them on a regular basis. This means that we have to make a conscious effort to form a bonding relationship with others. Our networks tend to be smaller and more task-driven, rather than help-driven. For those of you who are thinking that that is how they should be—small and focused on results—you have no idea how much money you are leaving on the table. Learn.

BRAIN SIZE—MINE'S BIGGER!

Women have always said that size doesn't matter. That's true, at least in terms of brain size. Female brain size is smaller than male's, but intellect is equal to or higher. But I know you already knew that.

Typically, men's brains are 11 to 12 percent larger than women's. This size difference has absolutely nothing to do with intelligence, but is explained by the difference in physical size between men and women. Men need more neurons to control their greater muscle mass and larger body size, so they have larger brains. Intellect is not about size. It's about white and gray matter, but we'll talk about that later. In this case, size doesn't matter. So don't be so proud.

PAIN

Women are also more likely to vocalize their pain and to seek treatment for it than are men. The area of the brain that is activated during pain is the amygdala. In women the left amygdala is activated, which has more connections with internal functions. This would also explain why women perceive pain more intensely than do men.

Men can deal with pain more easily than women and will not vocalize it very often. In men the right amygdala is activated which is connected with external functions.

I think what this really means is that women are tougher than men. When my wife gave birth to our first daughter, Jacqueline, I knew at that moment that women were stronger and tougher in every way. If men had to give birth we would have been extinct as a species many years ago.

Spatial Ability

Women have a thicker parietal region of the brain, which hinders the ability to mentally rotate objects—an aspect of spatial ability.

Men typically have stronger spatial abilities, (the mental abilities that let us envision a shape and its dynamics) whereas women typically struggle in this area.

When you hear women say, "I am so bad with directions. I always feel like I'm turned around and don't know where I am," this explains why. This may also be why men feel confident about directions. They NEVER stop and ask directions because they feel that they ALWAYS have it under control. NOT!

Susceptibility to Disorders

Women are more susceptible to mood disorders such as depression and anxiety. Men are more apt to have dyslexia or other language problems. Men are also more likely to be diagnosed with autism, ADHD, and Tourette's syndrome. (Does this mean I'm hard-wired to be hyperactive, confused by what I read, prone to yelling out obscenities, and unable to convey my feelings with words? How cool is that?!) Gentlemen, there's no arguing with brain research. Go be a man and be proud of your disorder! Seriously, let's see if we can work on this, OK?

⚲ She Says...
How Did You Learn Your Networking Skills?

I love this question, and it came out exactly as I would have expected it to, with women reading, taking seminars, and being mentored, and men just learning on their own. Ladies, are any of you one bit surprised that men scored highest in the category of "learned it on my own"? Men love to learn everything on their own. They get great joy and satisfaction from the achievement. Think about how many times you have watched your husband, father, or friend attempt to assemble some item on Christmas morning. Do they ever really take out the instructions and read them first? I remember when my husband assembled bicycles and was surprised at how many parts were left over. According to him, they must have been extras. Men want to figure things out on their own.

I was in a car with a gentleman and we were headed to an event. I asked him if he knew where we were going, and he said that he wasn't sure, but was pretty confident he could find it. "Where is your GPS?" I asked, and this is the response I got: "Oh, I only use that when my wife is with me. I really like trying to find places on my own and the GPS takes all the fun out of it. In fact, it is kind of like having my wife in the car, telling me how to get somewhere." I nearly fell to the floor laughing. "Don't you worry about being late or lost?" "No," he said, "I am pretty darn good at getting around this city and don't need someone telling me how to do it!" Men don't read instructions first. They just go for it. They turn to the instructions only if they really can't figure it out on their own. Don't get me wrong. There are women like that, too, and I'm one of them, but predominantly men are the ones who like to learn and accomplish things for themselves.

Men learn networking skills "on their own" at their fathers' knees from the day they are old enough to understand male bonding and relationship building. Participating in sports can be key in building networking relationships between men. They participate in sports as a player or spectator from a very early age. They do business on the golf course, and talk business in the bar over a beer while watching games. Their fraternities stay connected as a strong business network long after they've left school. They learn to network from all the men around them. That the statistics say they learn skills on their own is not surprising.

Comparatively speaking, women are new in the world of business and certainly in the world of sports. Our sororities were more about dating than connecting in the business world. Women do not tend to bond over sports and we don't have time to hang out in the bar or on the golf course. Things have changed a lot, but we still have a long way to go. We must teach our daughters the art of business networking and connecting to one another, and supporting and assisting each other to achieve the success that we all want to achieve.

In her book, *She Wins, You Win*, Gail Evans makes the following statement, "I realized like many women, I didn't want to play the game the way the guys did . . . . As time passed I also began to realize that one of the most important elements of the men's game was missing from the women's. Whatever you want to call it—support, teamwork, assistance, the bottom line was: The boys were all taking care of each other. The women weren't." Gail further states, "We help each other in the small picture, being supportive in times of trouble and giving advice about sticky job-related situations, but we are not helping over the big picture".

I go back to my original comment, which is that women are relatively new players in the field, only beginning to break through the world of business networking. Learning to network for women will not come from generations of women passing down secret skills from generation to generation. It will come from seeking out information.

When my children were small I stayed at home with them. I was involved with their schools and an active member of the PTA locally and statewide. One day, my husband had an accident that left him unable to work for a considerable amount of time. That meant there was no one to run the insurance agency that he started, and it was the sole source of our income. I suddenly had to leave the home and enter the world of business ownership. It didn't take me long to figure out that I needed to network if I was going to grow this business and help my family. In the beginning, I had no idea how to network, where to network, or who to network with. I was lost!

I began searching everywhere for classes, books, and people who could help me. The only book I could find at that time was *Endless Referrals* by Bob Burg. In his book he said to join networking groups, start connecting, and follow up to create more business. I read the book cover to cover and began to implement it into my business. I joined a closed-contact networking group called "The Network," later to become BNI. I joined the chamber of commerce and got on the ambassador committee and slowly but surely began to build a very substantial network. I spent a great deal of time seeking out more opportunities to learn how to network and took classes offered by local experts, read books, joined groups, and sought out others who could teach me how to network. At that time there were not many options to choose from.

Today I teach a lot of basic networking classes, and they are almost always filled with women. Whenever I ask the room what it is they want to get from the program, there is at least one woman in the room who says, "I was a stay-at-home mom before this and never had to network, so I just need to know how to do it".

Now more than ever, there are networking experts everywhere, along with blogs, books, and podcasts that all teach the art of networking. There are organizations like the Referral Institute that teach the deep skills of building business by referrals, as well as how to develop a successful network.

Of the 12,000 people who were surveyed, more than 91 percent of them said that networking played a role in their success. That shows how important it is to develop our skills. Developing a network and referral generating are not taught in most universities or schools. It is up to women to find the programs that best fit their needs and schedules. You have to learn more to earn more, and developing a strong network of contacts is key to many aspects of that, from finding jobs and making yourself highly visible to fulfilling your business needs.

Ladies, learning to build and leverage a strong network takes a lot of education, and none of us are born with a networking gene. Dr. Ivan Misner wrote a book called *The World's Best Known Marketing Secret*. How can something be best-known and still be a secret? We all know it is important, as you can see, and say it is part of our success, but there have been very few formal opportunities to learn the skills it takes not only to build a network, but to leverage it as well. Women are great at building networks, and now it's time to learn that it is OK to leverage them. Leveraging your network is a "Givers Gain®" activity, with both sides benefiting when we learn to do it well!

While men, indeed, do learn to network on their own, there is still much left for them to learn, too. Learning to develop stronger relationships that go beyond transactions, slowing down and building trust, and setting up systems that generate consistent business are things that men need to learn to do better. We all need to learn, but women just have a different starting point than men do.

Regardless of how much each of the sexes believes they know about networking there is always so much more to learn. Like anything else, networking, and referral systems are always evolving and we must continue to evolve, too, so that we can look back at women who are trying to learn and reach out a hand to mentor them, having just blazed the trail. We can teach our daughters the importance of networking. When our daughters go to school, leave home, go to college, and get jobs, they will have the advantage of having been taught the skills that are naturally passed on to boys. More women and moms are in the business world than ever before, and they should pass that business acumen on to their daughters as fathers do to their sons.

The Survey Says . . .
Attitude About Networking by Success

One of the findings from the study worth discussing involves attitudes about whether networking has played a role in respondents' success levels. The 95 percent of respondents who said that networking played a role in their success were at least somewhat to very comfortable with networking.

On the other hand, almost 70 percent of the respondents who said that networking had not played a role in their success were only somewhat comfortable to very uncomfortable.

It's hard to say whether it's the chicken or the egg with this finding. Do people who love to network achieve more success in their businesses? Or is it their success that fuels the comfort with the process of networking?

We've met people who say, "I want to get better at networking, but I'm just not very good at it." Isn't this really a self-fulfilling prophecy? How can you get better at something when you don't do it? To paraphrase my friend Michael Gerber in the *E-Myth Seminar*, "You don't try to get people to feel motivated so they'll do better. People feel more motivated as a result of doing better." We are inclined to agree: The behavior is more likely to fuel the success than the success fueling the behavior. In other words, the more you do something, the better you get at it. That applies to playing a musical instrument, competing in a sport, or networking for business. You can't win the game if you don't practice. And if you don't practice, you won't get better—which means you won't like it. This frustrating cycle can be broken by looking at an activity's components and identifying which elements feel enjoyable. If people focus on the aspects of networking that they like, they'll do it more—and thus enjoy more success. For example, here's one man who teams up with his wife because he believes she is so good at the process it improves his success at it:

My wife does a lot of networking for me. She is really good about starting conversations, and after she warms the person up, she introduces me. I then continue the conversation to build the relationship. My wife is also very good about following up with people, and then bringing me in again and again.

On the other hand, here's a comment from a woman who identifies her emotional intelligence as being important to her success in networking:

Being able to develop a good relationship initially helps me understand how to best work with someone else in business. Having this emotional intelligence is my strength, and I can help others get their needs met. That in itself helps me meet my own needs.

♂ He Says . . .

This is pretty simple. As adults, all we are is big kids. If we don't like something, we don't want to do it. If we enjoy a particular activity, we wish to do it more. Because we enjoy it, we focus on it and want to get better at it. This is the same with men and networking for business. Men who enjoy it will do it more, and become better at it. The more often they do it and the higher their level of skill, the greater results they will achieve. The greater their results, the more inspired they are, and the more motivated they become to continue and create greater success.

If we look at the adult learner, we know that both men and women alike will enjoy learning more when they are engaged in the process. Andragogy is the art of teaching to adults. In order for adults to want to learn, the teachings must be problem-centered rather than content-centered; permit and encourage active participation; encourage the use of past experiences; be collaborative between instructor-student and student-student; be based on planning between the teacher and the learner; be based on an evaluation agreement; and incorporate experiential activities. Why do I mention all this now? Because if we are looking at the behavior of our networkers and saying that the behavior drives the success, then the behavior of learning will drive greater success.

 # She Says . . .

Have you ever met anyone who had a bad attitude about what they were doing and at the same time was highly successful at it? We become successful at the things we believe we can become successful at.

How do we become successful at anything we do? By doing it correctly? One of the statistics in our study shows that people who enjoy networking also spend more time doing it, have developed systems for tracking results, and spend more time working their networks.

Think about when you learned to ride a bike, roller skate, ski, or knit for example. Were you good at it the very first time you tried it? I remember when I got my very first bicycle, my grandparents bought it for me, and my grandfather helped me get on the bike. It had little training wheels, and for several days I wobbled around the neighborhood. After the third day, my grandfather took the training wheels off and ran alongside me as I struggled to maintain balance and stay upright. Finally, he let go of me, and I was riding on my own. After that, I skinned my knees and elbows, crashed into things, and had a bunch of accidents, but kept riding because I loved it. I never considered that I couldn't do it or quitting. I just kept riding. Today, I still ride my bike. I love riding it, and am very good at it, but it required that I skin my knees a few times to get to this point.

Networking is the same way. You get out there and do it, and aren't so good at it when you start, but don't quit. Read articles and books, take classes, get a mentor, hire a coach, and keep networking. Every time you have some success, your attitude will get better and your success will increase. It doesn't matter if you're male or female. The better attitude you have, the more success you generate, and the more success you generate, the better your attitude will be about networking.

3

Communication
Transaction
vs. Relationship

The Survey Says . . .
The Process of Visibility,
Credibility, and Profitability

In order to appreciate some of the results of the survey that we discuss throughout the book, it is important to have an understanding of a concept I call the VCP Process®. Although the VCP Process® isn't actually part of the survey, it is the foundation for our analysis of several aspects of the survey throughout this book.

When business professionals develop relationships, there are two different orders that usually take place, depending on the preference of the person. The first is to do business together first, then later work on the relationship. The second is to focus on nurturing the relationship and then begin doing business together. We wanted to know which style professionals prefer and what they are actually motivated by at networking functions when deciding their *modus operandi*. This preference by gender was one of the questions we most wanted our survey to answer, because as specialists in referral marketing we believe that the VCP Process® is the key to building relationships, and personal relationships are the foundation of a powerful business referral network.

An understanding of the VCP Process® is critical to an evaluation of these two factors. Any effective referral marketing plan involves relationships of many different kinds. Among the most important are those that professionals have with their referral sources, the prospects those referral partners bring to them, and the customers they recruit from the prospects.

These relationships don't just spring up fully developed; they must be nurtured and tended to over time. They start out tentative, fragile, full of unfulfilled possibilities and expectations, and then grow stronger with experience and familiarity, finally maturing into trust and commitment. As they grow they're fed by mutual trust and shared benefits, which allow them to evolve through the three critical phases of visibility, credibility, and profitability. This evolution is what I call the VCP Process®.

Visibility

In this first phase of growing a relationship, each of the players in the social circle becomes aware of the other(s). In business terms, a potential source of referrals or a potential customer becomes aware of the nature of your business, perhaps because of your public relations and advertising efforts, or perhaps through a mutual connection. This person may observe you in the act of conducting business or relating with the people around you. The two of you begin to communicate and establish a connection or perhaps explore a question or two over the phone about product availability. You may become personally acquainted and work together on a first-name basis, but know little about one another. A combination of many such relationships forms a casual-contact network, a sort of de facto association based on one or more shared interests.

The visibility phase is important because it creates recognition and awareness. The greater your visibility, the more widely known you'll become. The more information you gather about others, the more opportunities you'll be privy to and your public profile will grow accordingly, allowing you greater opportunities for being accepted and thought of when referral time comes. Visibility must be actively maintained and developed; without it, it's impossible to graduate to the next level.

Credibility

Establishing credibility requires an initiation period that proves your professional credo is reliable and worthy of confidence. Once you and your new acquaintance begin to form expectations of each other that are fulfilled a few times, your relationship can enter the credibility stage. If both parties are gaining satisfaction from the relationship in a continual flow, then it appears that satisfaction will continue, and the relationship begins to strengthen with its new determined value.

Credibility grows when appointments and promises are kept, facts are verified, and services are rendered in full or beyond. The phrase "going the distance" comes to mind as an illustration of proving all of the elements required within the definition of a top-quality service provider. The old saying that actions speak louder than words is true. What you do is more important than what you say you will do, and you can't go wrong if you set the bar at 110 percent instead of just meeting your quota. Failure to live up to expectations or keep explicit and implicit promises can kill a budding relationship before it has a chance to bloom; this kind of negative visibility has the potential to follow you around for a long time.

To determine your credibility, people often turn to a third party who's either known you longer or done business with you. They may ask whether or not that person would recommend you, if you're honest, if your product is of quality, and if you come through on deadlines.

A chain is only as strong as its weakest link. When evaluating and taking inventory of your VCP relationships, remember that they are two-sided and only as strong as both of you agree. The combination of your perception with theirs doesn't average out any difference in feelings. For example, if you've moved your relationship with Bill into the credibility stage, but Bill feels you are still in the visibility stage, then that's where you'll stay until both parties feel the love. You'd need to classify this relationship at visibility-level status until things improve in the eyes of both parties and take you to the next level.

Profitability

The mature relationship, whether business or personal, can be defined in terms of its profitability. Is it mutually rewarding? Do both partners gain satisfaction from it? Does it maintain its status and value by providing benefits to both? If it doesn't profit both partners, it probably will disintegrate.

The time it takes a relationship to pass through these development phases is highly variable. In some relationships profitability will be achieved in a week, others in a month or even a year, and it's not always easy to predict. In a time of urgency, there may be the opportunity for both parties to quickly rise to the occasion and complete daunting deadlines. After such a dramatic, challenging project, you both may proceed from visibility to credibility overnight, having shown one another quickly what may normally take years to reveal. The same is true of profitability; it may happen quickly, or take years, depending on the circumstances and opportunities available to show your colors. Most relationships fall somewhere in between, toting the gradual, bit-by-bit, accumulative process of working together on many smaller jobs until confidence is earned and realized. The either rapid or slow forward development is most affected by the motivation and desire of both parties to please one another, as well as the frequency and quality of the referrals they contribute.

Shortsightedness can impede full development of the relationship. Perhaps you're a customer who has done business with a certain vendor intermittently for several months, but to save pennies you keep hunting around for the lowest price, ignoring the vendor's true value of top-notch service, generous goodwill, and unwavering reliability and availability. In continuing to focus on lowering your cost, are you really profiting from the relationship, or stunting its growth? Perhaps if you gave this vendor all your business, you could work out terms that would benefit both of you.

REMEMBER THE BUMPER STICKER "QUESTION REALITY"?

Think creatively and never be afraid to approach redefining your relationships. You may get a pleasant surprise. You determine your world! Don't let gravity take control.

It's important to note that this is a referral process, not a sales process. You might be in the profitability phase with a client in terms of selling them your products or services, but if you aren't getting regular referrals from them, you're not in that phase of the VCP Process®. In order for that to happen, they need to think that your service model is so wonderful that others should know about you, too.

The Survey Says...
Relationships First

In our experience the three phases of visibility, credibility, and profitability are key to forming a mature networking relationship. Both the men and women in our survey reaffirmed our belief that a good relationship is the prerequisite for a mutually beneficial referral business, and not the other way around. Men seem to relate to and get their identity from their businesses much more so than women do.

Actress and fitness instructor Nicole Brandon relates a story that reflects that tendency. She was working out at a gym when a man asked if she was an exercise trainer, to which she replied, "Yes." He then asked if she could help him with the exercise equipment, because it was all new to him. She said that of course, she'd be glad to help and asked what he did. He said that he was the vice president of XYZ company and directed all the marketing for the organization.

She said, "No, I meant, what do you do in your exercise routine!"

Men most often present themselves by what they do. It's how they relate.

The Transactional vs. Relational Approach

In this survey we asked people if they preferred the transactional approach to networking, focusing on business first and then on the relationship, or the relational networking approach, first building the relationship and then the business. The vast majority of respondents preferred to first build a relationship then focus on the business. However, when you compare the preferences by gender, an interesting result emerges. Within the minority of people who considered it better to focus on the business first, men outnumbered women by almost 53 percent to roughly 47 percent (see Figure 3.1). Conversely, the women outnumbered men by a small, but statistically significant number in their preference for focusing on the relationship first. This observation from one of our respondents lends insight on preferred networking styles:

> I attended a breakfast event. When I arrived, I joined a group of businessmen who within a very short time were exchanging business cards. I then sat at a table of businesswomen. They talked about the speaker and conversed, getting to know each other a little better. Before they left, each woman at the table exchanged cards. They achieved the same results, with different timing. The men got straight to business first, whereas the women wanted to get to know the other person before they exchanged cards.

When networking for business I believe			
	It is better to focus on business and build a relationship later.	It is better to build a relationship first then focus on the business.	Response Totals
Female	47.4% (724)	**50.5% (4,810)**	**50.1% (5,534)**
Male	**52.6% (803)**	49.5% (4,718)	50.5% (5,521)
Answered question	1,527	9,526	**11,053**
Skipped question			2

FIGURE 3.1—**Gender Preferences for Networking Focus**

Going into this study, my co-authors and I had a working hypothesis about the VCP Process® and gender. We believed that women might have a tendency to get tangled and hung up in the transition between the visibility and credibility phases. We thought that women might be prone to linger in the credibility phase longer, procrastinating moving to the profitability phase, where they'd have to be asking for referrals and business. We also felt that men were more likely to try and skip right over that middle stage and jump straight from visibility to profitability.

The indication that women, by however small a margin, seem to put more emphasis on the relationship is no great surprise. Is it possible that women tend to move through the VCP Process® from visibility to credibility and get delayed there, whereas men jump the gun and try to circumvent the middle phase, shooting straight from visibility to profitability? The data gives us a glimmer of support on this presumption, but perhaps the comments and polar gender perspectives of Frank and Hazel will shed more light.

♂ He Says . . .

It seems that most men and women believe in the concept of Ivan's VCP Process® and understand that its contribution to building strong business relationships relies on going through each of its phases in order. Both sexes think, "Hey, VCP, yes, that's what I do!" but women are the only ones really practicing it.

Fellas, do we really think we are building credibility this fast? As usual, we are jumping ahead prematurely, going straight to the profitability phase. Can I tell you how hard it is to admit to our faults over and over? It's especially difficult with Hazel looking over my shoulder and rubbing my nose in it every time. Guys, help me out here . . . please!

Men are pretty good at becoming publicly visible. We're driven to make a statement, get our names and presence out into the world, and let people know what we do. It doesn't mean the visibility phase is enjoyable or comfortable for us, but shining the spotlight on ourselves is a bit akin to tooting our own horns, and we've all seen evidence that men are more at ease with this aspect of self-promotion than women, as voiced in this responder's comment:

> I teach men and women in a workshop called "How to Love Networking." The most common gender-related generalization my research shows is that women are uniquely talented at creating and sustaining relationships naturally and are also the most challenged when it comes to making a request. Men tend to think in more linear terms and are more outcomes focused.

She Comments . . .

Yes, I've seen you strut! That's where the expression "cock of the walk" comes from.

He Responds . . .

Yes, we do tend to strut, and sometimes there's nothing but hot air behind a façade while at others there's real content and credibility, but the problem lies in not taking the time to evolve through the credibility phase so that women can see our worth.

We're under the illusion that we've established credibility by self-promotion and then think that of course, next will come profitability and the closing of deals.

Let's talk about what we men consider "credibility." When questioning an acquaintance's credibility, have you had someone respond sarcastically with something like: "Of course they're the best in the area. I know they are because they told me." I'm certainly guilty of claiming this on occasion, but when I step back and listen to how that sounds, I realize how ridiculous it seems to think that confidence is gained by just telling people how fantastic, wonderful, smart, charming, talented, and incredible I am.

She Comments . . .

I'm pretty sure most women reading this can recall at least a few dates they've been on where the guys have had no problem talking about themselves for the duration of the evening.

He Responds . . .

Hey, I resent that! I will admit, though, it's a good analogy in that on a date, it would certainly be ridiculous for the woman to base whether to continue dating the guy on what he merely bragged up about himself. Most women want to see what a guy actually does and how he follows through before deciding to take him seriously as relationship material, or not.

I guess I'm not being entirely accurate in saying that method doesn't work. It does work with men who do the same thing. Boy, is that something to watch. The battle of the egos! Entertainment aside, we're not trying to get men to work better with men, are we? We're trying to help men work more effectively with women.

The first rule to networking effectively with women is: Don't talk about your credentials! Stop trying to impress women by displaying your accomplishments. For women, credibility comes from the building of a relationship during which they'll see over time all the things you're restraining yourself from bragging about. One good reason why this is a better way to get to believe in someone is that when you see someone act repeatedly on their stated beliefs and work ethic it becomes a solid fact with underlying proof.

Another reason, in case you forgot, is that a relationship is a two-way street. That means that you should care about the other person and they should know by your actions that you do. I don't mean you should care at the level of taking a bullet for them. I'm just suggesting that you try to get to know them by asking questions and taking an interest in their lives. Women want to know that they're more than just a transaction to you. This respondent has it figured out:

Networking with men is different than with women. With men I am short and sweet in my communications. With women I get more into asking lots of questions and finding out about them and their families.

TIP

Make it your business to genuinely care about other people, and you'll become an asset to them, which gets you ahead in the credibility phase. Credibility IS your sale.

This influences your credibility with women. If you wonder why they need more than your verbal professional bio, you're not looking at it from their perspective. Much like in marketing and sales, the kind of person you present yourself as and how you treat your client often holds more water than the product you're selling. If they think of you as a pushy, insincere jerk, or someone who's not concerned about what's good for them, you can forget about the sale. The same thinking holds true here. Credibility IS the sale.

The bottom line is that if you focus on what women want and give it to them, they'll love you forever. It's pretty simple. But to do this, you need to care about understanding them and the way they think. Ah, such mysterious and wonderful creatures, women.

Think about how happy your significant other would be if you helped her with everything that made her life easier, before she asked you to. For her, it would feel like a wonderful fantasy in which you had the ability to read her mind and give her what she wanted. She'd never have to ask you to do anything again. Imagine never having to say, "How was I supposed to know you wanted me to do that? You never asked me!" Imagine never again having to hear her disappointed response, "I shouldn't have to ask. You should just know!"

Which Way Is Best, Relationships First or Business First?

This respondent's comment really sums up some of our core networking differences:

> Men seem to be more hesitant to build deep relationships and women tend to focus too much on everything but business.

It's no amazing revelation to say that the first priority for women is relationships, and for men, getting business. DNA evidence and the roles men still play in our society support that fact. Men have been the hunters, protectors, and providers of our clans since the beginning of time. This is not to say female breadwinners are not increasing in number every day as the sole supporters of their families, because they are. But let's go back to who we are at a primal level.

As the provider, I feel it is my responsibility to bring home the bacon, steak, buffalo—or squirrel, if it has been a very bad day. When I'm bringing that catch home, I'm not trying to build a forever relationship with that meal that I'm hunting. I need to catch it, prepare it for my family, and get it home, just like the sales and deals I go after in today's world.

Unfortunately, we men approach everyone in our networks as if they were our next meal to be slain, because we see the processes the same. Today we have to learn to be more relational and less transactional and plant seeds, like women do, that will provide us with continued business over and over as the years go by.

Most men in business who are involved in sales are very aware of the importance of relationships. But the relationships we instinctively prioritize are the transaction-related ones. My goal is not to create best friends from my business networks. It is to develop relationships that are beneficial to me. I'm not saying this is a good thing or the way it should be. I am just stating that this is the way it is. I must provide for my family, and my instincts tell me to take care of my own first. This is what we men do and are generally pretty successful at it, but we must continue to learn as we have for millions of years to keep current with new technology and methods. We must learn to adapt so that we can be more successful in less time and with less effort.

One of our strengths is staying focused on the sale, closing deals, and the hunt. However, we're seeing that our transaction-related relationships are not working with women who are relationship oriented and not at all focused on transactions as their primary objective. We are losing to those male hunters who have decided to communicate in more female ways.

Women have been the gatherers and community builders for as long as we have been hunters. By building a sense of community they created a nurturing environment for the children and a place for the community to share its riches. Part of the job of gatherers is to collect plants and herbs needed for nutritional and healing purposes. As our tribes discovered the benefits of plant life as food, women began to nurture gardens and small farms.

The act of planting and caring for seeds to grow plants mirrors the building of relationships.

First you plant the seeds. You then care for and protect them, making sure they are planted deep enough and consistently watered over time. You monitor their growth until they are ready to be harvested, and give you back all the work, or investment, you've put into them.

Male contributions to the tribe, like shooting a buffalo, happen in a matter of minutes, whereas the female contributions, like growing food, require tending for months. That's quite a difference. Women have understood for thousands of years the benefit and importance of developing mutually beneficial relationships. Modern times find them using those same instincts and skill sets to develop business relationships.

When women network they are working as gatherers, planting seeds and acquiring friends, not just using transactional friends the way men do, but actual friends. They care about and are interested in their friends and want to help them and talk to them. Yikes! This is scary stuff for men.

So what does all this mean? Men need to become more adept at building real relationships. The problem with a transactional relationship is that it is based on the transaction. Once the transaction is over, then the relationship is over. Women, on the other hand, would do well to focus on extracting more transactions from their business friendships. They must keep in mind what the purpose of business networking is.

Building strong relationships starts by examining how we communicate with one another. It's very different from the way women do. I know that that isn't news to anyone.

First let's define what we mean by communication. Communication is a combination of the verbal and nonverbal details you emit with your choice of words, mannerisms, clothing and style, and grooming habits. All of this communicates who you are and what you stand for.

Both sexes communicate with each other using codes. The group of friends we are speaking with dictates the communication style we use. With close friends the conversations are straightforward, in an "anything goes" style, and with more distant acquaintances they are more professional and reserved. Both men and women adjust communication styles according to the company they're in. This is a natural process and not one we necessarily do consciously.

Yes, there are those that do not know how to adjust their communication style to the crowd they are in. These people tend to alienate themselves. They are what we call "social misfits." They just don't get it. They haven't been trained and/or don't have the innate skills to observe and learn socially acceptable behavior. Either their parents didn't teach them or they lack the sensitivity to observe and learn it from somewhere else. At any rate, parents, this is an invaluable skill to teach your children.

We've all met that guy at a social function whose favorite topic is him. Through the entire conversation you both express interest in him and if he does ask about you or your business it's obviously only out of obligation. When you ask about him, he eagerly jumps in headfirst, excited to educate you all about his fascinating world. It's everything you never wanted to know, and he's trying to sell to you the whole way through. That guy also has an inclination to tell off-color jokes and comment inappropriately to women about their clothing and looks.

He's actually harmless and not trying to hurt anyone or be rude. He's just clueless. Most of us just put up with him and then roll our eyes when he moves on to the next person or group. We then smile at one another with a sly comment and continue talking as if he never existed.

There's something important that that guy teaches me. I don't ever want to be the person that people laugh at, smirk over, or roll their eyes and snidely talk about. That guy is a wrecking ball, destroying potential relationships left and right. The damage his clumsy social blunders cause lasts a long time and can be very difficult to get past.

One of the things Mr. Social Misfit is really good at not doing is adapting his communication style to those around him. Most of us do this instinctively and subconsciously. We don't try to adapt, we just do. Let me give you an example with this story of Little Johnny and Mr. Henderson.

Little Johnny Meets a New Friend

Little Johnny is three years old, and his father introduces him to his friend Mr. Henderson. Mr. Henderson, in his great stature, stands at six feet four inches and weighs in at 230 pounds. His gray hair and booming voice command deference.

Johnny's dad calls out, "Johnny, I would like you to meet Mr. Henderson, the president of the bank."

Mr. Henderson sees Johnny, puts out his hand, and says in his strong corporate president voice, "Hello, Johnny. I'm Hank Henderson. It's a pleasure to meet you."

Johnny, who looks like a frightened puppy, says, "Huh?"

"So Johnny, tell me, what were your activities today and what do you have planned for tomorrow?" asks Mr. Henderson.

Three-year-old Johnny says, "I dunno."

"Well, Johnny, it's important to have goals in your life. What do you want to accomplish in the next year?" Mr. Henderson asks with great anticipation.

Johnny looks confused and starts to say something but can't. He just tears up and then cries and runs away.

Mr. Henderson looks confused and says to Johnny's dad, "You're going to have to get him focused and give him a little backbone."

What was the problem with this conversation? Did Mr. Henderson, bank president, speak to Johnny as if he were a 3- or 30-year-old? He didn't adapt his communication style appropriately and spoke to the toddler the same way he speaks to adults.

Little Johnny Makes a New Friend: Take Two

Let's look at the next scenario and see what happens when Mr. Henderson approaches Johnny differently.

Johnny's dad calls him into the room saying, "Johnny, this is Mr. Henderson, the president of the bank."

Mr. Henderson crouches down to try and get almost eye-level with Johnny and says, "Hey, Johnny. I'm Hank. Wow, that's a really cool Sponge Bob shirt you have on. I love Sponge Bob. Do you like Sponge Bob?"

Johnny smiles, "Uh-huh," and points to Sponge Bob on his shirt.

"Johnny, how old are you? Five?" Mr. Henderson asks, knowing that Johnny is three.

Johnny smiles again and says, "No, I'm free," and holds up three fingers.

"Three! You can't be three. You are way too big to be three. You look like you're five. Are you sure you're three?" says Mr. Henderson with great surprise in his voice.

"Yup. I'm only free." He beams proudly, very impressed that someone thinks he is big enough to be five.

"Well, you are a big boy and very smart, I can see. It is great meeting you," says Mr. Henderson in his friendliest voice.

"You wanna come play wif me?" Johnny asks of his new friend.

What happened here? Mr. Henderson adapted his communication style to the person he was speaking with and won his affection. I'm sure you've either done this or have seen others do it. It's the only way to win over children in the beginning.

Does the same thing work with adults? Absolutely.

In order to communicate more effectively and quickly form a relationship that opens up maximum potential, your communication style has to make the other person feel comfortable. The question is, are you currently doing this with members of the opposite sex? Are you being flexible and adaptable in your communication style, or are you just doing what's comfortable for you without regard to adapting to what other people may like? Men and women communicate very differently. Therefore it is up to each sex to adapt to the other's style. This will form quick and strong bonds.

Men, this is what we need to do in our conversations with women, not in a condescending or patronizing way, but sincerely, with the goal of developing a relationship. This goes for ANY type of relationship. Some people do this naturally and some don't. If we want to create meaningful relationships in business, this is where we must begin. We must make a conscious effort to adapt our style and that will allow us to bond through communication.

Why We Act the Way We Do

Dr. Deborah Tannen conducted a behavioral communication study of young boys and girls to see how they would act when asked to just have a conversation while being videotaped. The boys were extremely uncomfortable with this request, while the girls of all ages had no problem with it. Immediately the girls faced each other and started talking, which led to a conversation about one of their problems.

Boys, on the other hand, sat parallel to each other and jumped from topic to topic. The topics all related to making plans to "do" something together. For boys, activities, doing things together, are central. Just sitting and talking is not an essential part of friendship. Boys are friends with the boys they do things with.

Females, on the other hand, use conversation to create closeness and intimacy; for females, conversation is the essence of intimacy, so being best friends means sitting and talking.

It is important for women to understand that male communication is all about status. Think about all those nature shows you've seen on PBS. The prime goal of male beasties is mating; and to do this they must be powerful enough to challenge the lead males in the herd. As they grow up, they bide their time until mating by establishing a pecking order. When a beastie is big and strong enough to have most of the other males "under" him, he is ready to take on the "old man." If he wins the fight, he gets to mate with the females of his choice (and they will mate only with him). Human males act in the exact same way.

This dynamic is important to remember when looking at another major area of miscommunication between men and women. Women cannot understand the resistance men seem to have when asked for assistance or consideration of some kind or another. Women must remember the above scenario and understand that when men do what they're asked to do, it means they have lost status in that relationship. Men often feel that women are trying to manipulate them. What a woman might see as a simple request is seen by her man as an attempt to manipulate him into a "one-down" position.

Dr. Tannen elaborates, "Women want men to do what we want. If a woman perceives that something she's doing is really hurting a man, she wants to stop doing it. If she perceives that he really wants her to do something, she wants to do it. She thinks that that's love and he should feel the same way about her. But men have a gut-level resistance to doing what they're told, to doing what someone expects them to do. It's the opposite response of what women have." She reminds readers that, of course, there are also men out there who are very helpful toward their women.

In sharp contrast to the communication style of men, which seeks to establish and maintain status and dominance, women's communicating is more egalitarian, or rule-by-consensus-oriented. When women get together they seek the input of the other women present and make decisions based on the wishes of the group.

What this means in the business world is that each sex, at the core of our being, is a different animal when it comes to communication. You are speaking giraffe and I am speaking lion. We men may understand the general message and tone of what you are saying, but the specifics—fuggedaboudit! We have no clue. Yes, ladies I am talking to you, too, when I suggest we all put away our giraffe and lion talk when we are together, and instead speak a common language. That common language isn't too familiar to either sex, but I know we can make it work well if we both try. Remember during all of this that the goal is about bond, rapport, trust, and confidence.

First There Was IQ and EQ; Now There Is GQ

Ladies, we are simple creatures. Keep it short, simple, and to the point. Here are some great tips for communicating with "the hunters."

1. Speak directly and to a point. Get right to the goal of the conversation and don't talk around it. We hate circular conversations. We love targeted, direct conversations that go from point A to point B without detours.

2. If you have a question, ask it.

3. If you have a need, ask for what you need.

4. Understand that MEN DO NOT KNOW what WOMEN are thinking. Not only do we not know, we don't even have the tiniest hint of a clue. We are not the brightest when it comes to you women and

what you want. You've heard of IQ and EQ, right? We've now also established GQ: The Gender Quotient. This is the measure of one's level of intelligence about the opposite sex. This quotient came from studies of more than 10 billion men over the last 100 years and has shown that on a scale from 1 to 10 (1 meaning a man is virtually dead and hardly knows the female species exists or recognizes any differences between the genders, and 10 meaning the man's communication level is equivalent to a woman's true soul mate).

Overall men averaged a strong 1.278 when it came to understanding women. Unabashedly, we are VERY proud that we scored that high. Women, on the other hand, averaged 4.00001. OK, you're a little better we are, but don't be so proud. You don't really understand us very well either. (You do realize that these numbers are made up, as is the study. But you get my point, right?) Fake study or not, I want to assure you that the newly founded GQ is here to stay.

Here are some examples of how the difference in GQ manifests itself in everyday interactions between men and women:

When she says:	"It's your decision."
We think she means:	"It's my decision."
What she actually means is:	"You'd better know what I really want and give it to me right now."
When she says:	"Go ahead and do what you want."
We think she means:	"It's OK with her if I do what I want."
What she actually means:	"I don't want you to, and you're going to pay for this later."
When she says:	"I don't care what a man looks like, as long as he's a nice guy."
We think she means:	"Providing he's got lots of money and a status job so my girlfriends will be jealous of me, I will like him, regardless of his looks."

What she actually means:	Exactly what we thought. Shame on you, ladies! We men would never be so shallow as to like a woman just because she has a gorgeous face, great body, blonde hair, large trust fund, and doesn't speak English. Never!

What About Networking GQ?

Tips on working with us:

1. Don't talk to us about a problem. Ask us how to solve it. We don't want to talk about it. We want to impress you with our problem-solving aptitude.

2. If you ask us to help you solve a problem because you don't know what to do, don't tell us we are wrong and that there's a better way to do it after we tell you how to do it. Hey, if you already knew the answer, why the heck did you ask us?

3. Don't come to us moody or depressed. Remain even-tempered and logical. Please watch Star Trek and study Mr. Spock. Model his communication style and way of thinking.

4. Don't assume we mean something different than what we said. If I say, "I like your hair," don't respond, "Why? Didn't it look nice before? How about the shoes? Why didn't you say anything about the shoes? Why don't you like the shoes?"

A big part of this problem is that women feel men don't and can't communicate. Actually, men can communicate, and do, quite clearly, in fact. It appears as though our straightforwardness is our downfall.

From the man's point of view, less is more. Why use ten words when you can use two? We think women are communication handicapped because they just keep talking and never really get to the point of what they began the dialogue with in the first place.

Women, stop expecting men to communicate like you do. We don't and won't. We may try, but understand that it is not our natural style to do so.

Men, have a real conversation. Stop giving two-word answers. Practice active listening.

Funny but True

This scenario is a true classic. Ladies and gentlemen, I dare you to read this and tell me it's not typical. Bet you can't.

Bill asks Candace out on a date. They have a great time. They then start to date regularly.

Six months later, while driving home from their dinner date Candace says, "Do you realize that tonight is our six-month anniversary?" For a few seconds, there is silence in the car, and to Candace it seems like hours of deafening silence. She thinks to herself, I wonder if it bothers him that I said that. Maybe he's been feeling confined by our relationship. Maybe he thinks I'm trying to push him into some kind of obligation that he doesn't want, or isn't sure of.

Meanwhile, Bill is thinking, Hmmm, six months.

Candace is percolating away in her head with, But, hey, I'm not so sure I want this kind of relationship, either. Sometimes I wish I had a little more space, so I'd have time to think about whether I really want us to keep going the way we are, moving steadily forward. Where are we going with this thing, anyway? Are we just going to keep seeing each other at this level of intimacy? Are we heading toward marriage? Children? An entire lifetime together? Am I ready for that level of commitment? Do I really even know this person?

At this point Bill is thinking, So that means it was . . . let's see . . . February when we started going out, which was right after I had the car at the dealer's, which means . . . lemme check the odometer . . . Whoa! I'm way overdue for an oil change!

Candace is now at the point where she's thinking, He's upset. I can see it on his face. Maybe I'm reading this completely wrong. Maybe he wants more from our relationship, more intimacy, more commitment. Maybe he's sensed, even before I did, that I had some reservations. Yes, I'll bet that's it. That's why he's so reluctant to say anything about his own feelings. He's afraid of being rejected.

Bill is thinking, Yeah, and I'm gonna have them look at the transmission again. I don't care what those morons say, it's still not shifting right. And they better not try to blame it on the cold weather this time. What cold weather? It's 87 degrees out, and this thing is shifting like a garbage truck, and I paid those incompetent thieves $600.

Candace is thinking, He's angry. And I don't blame him. I'd be angry, too. I feel so guilty, putting him through this, but I can't help the way I feel. I'm just not sure.

Bill is thinking, They'll probably say it's only a 90-day warranty. That's exactly what they're gonna say, the scum.

Candace is thinking, Maybe I'm just too idealistic, waiting for a knight to come riding up on his white horse when I'm sitting right next to a perfectly good person, a person I enjoy being with, truly do care about, and who seems to truly care about me. And now this person is in pain because of my self-centered, schoolgirl romantic fantasy.

Bill is thinking, Warranty? They want a warranty? I'll give them a warranty. I'll take their warranty and . . .

"Bill." Candace says aloud.

"What?" answers Bill, startled.

"Please don't torture yourself like this." she says, her eyes beginning to brim with tears, "Maybe I should never have . . . Oh, I feel so . . ."

She breaks down, sobbing.

"What?" Bill asks, wondering what just happened.

"I'm such a fool." Candace sobs. "I mean, I know there's no knight. I really know that. It's silly. There's no knight, and there's no horse."

"There's no horse?" says Bill and wonders, What horse?

"You think I'm a fool, don't you?" Candace asks in a self-blaming tone.

"No!" says Bill, thinking, Why should I?

"It's just that . . . it's that I . . . I need some time," Candace says.

Dead silence again. Bill is trying to find what the right answer is here. Finally he comes up with one that he thinks might work.

"Yes," he says.

Candace feels so touched that she puts her hand on his.

"Oh, Bill, do you really feel that way?" she says.

"What way?" says Bill, thinking, What are we talking about?

"That way about time?" asks Candace.

"Oh," says Bill. "Yes. Of course."

Candace turns to face him and gazes deeply into his eyes, causing him to become very nervous about what she might say next, especially if it involves a horse. At last she speaks.

"Thank you, Bill," she says, lovingly.

"Thank you," says Bill, thinking, Whew. Got that one right.

Then he drops her off at her house where she lies and weeps on her bed, a conflicted, tortured soul, whereas Bill back at his place opens a bag of Doritos, turns on the TV, and immediately becomes deeply involved in a rerun of a tennis match between two Czechoslovakians he's never heard of.

A tiny voice in the far recesses of his mind tells him that something major was going on back there in the car, but he's pretty sure there is no way he would ever understand what, so he figures it's better if he doesn't think about it.

Candace gets home and calls her closest friend and they talk about this situation for two hours. They analyze everything she said and everything he said, going over it many times, considering every word, expression, and gesture for nuances of meaning, and any possible ramifications. They'll continue to discuss this subject, off and on, for weeks, maybe even months, never reaching any definite conclusions, but never getting bored with it, either.

Meanwhile, Bill, while playing basketball one day with a mutual friend of his and Candace's, stops before shooting a basket and says, 'Steve, did Candace ever own a horse?"

Taking Responsibility for How We Present Ourselves

You may remember the man in Chapter 1 who was very impressed with himself for cockily squeezing a woman's behind at a networking meeting, trying to impress his friends. Men need to take responsibility for how they act. In what universe would this be appropriate? Ladies, on behalf of men everywhere, I apologize for that guy. Here's a quote from one of our male study participants that also shows some irresponsible preoccupations guys have that get in the way of progress for everyone:

> When I network with a woman I always wonder what their marital status is first and foremost. I've no idea why, as I'm happily married myself and have nothing to gain from this curiosity. This can be distracting. It would be much easier if, when introducing themselves, they told me their marital status as well, then we could get down to business.

Let me get this right. You're married and distracted by not knowing if the female you've met is married or not? Really? This is not only strange, but also creepy. Ladies, here I go again, having to apologize for my team.

These examples are really embarrassing, and those few clueless men ruin it for the rest of us. To them I say that if you want the kind of strong reputation a true professional has, then earn it by acting like a professional! Now for a little peer pressure: To those of you who've got your act on track, coach the guys who don't have a clue, because their behavior affects all of us.

Some of us men just don't understand that when we're networking, we're always being observed and judged. Even by our buddies. Here is my question to you: How many close friendships that you have developed through networking do you actually get business from? For many of us the answer is: very little. Have you ever wondered why? One of the reasons could be that although your buddies have a great time with you, they are not confident enough in you to refer you. You may be fun to have a beer with, but referring you to their best client or family member or close friend is not going to happen.

I want you to have the mindset that each time you attend a networking function, of any kind, that you're auditioning. Business people are always looking for a reason to say "no." The most recent impression you give people during an audition is the way they think of you right now. Did you know that casting directors who audition people for movies and TV shows repeatedly request to audition many of the same actors? This repetition and visibility helps them remember the actor's persona. How you audition builds your credibility and reputation for certain types of roles for which people are "casting." When a role comes up that a prospective job hunter thinks you'd be good for, they'll make sure you attend the casting call to audition you again, even though they've seen you before. They need to see you audition for this role in your current status to make a decision about whether to recommend you.

The opposite is also true. When certain roles come up for which they don't think you'd be good, based on past auditions, they won't invite you. If you end up auditioning for them, they've usually already made their decision based on your performance at past auditions, so it's probably just a waste of time. Don't blow your opportunity to be invited to future auditions.

Gentlemen, if you want to network well and build relationships with women, you need to make sure, every time you see them, you treat it like your first audition. Make each impression count. It could be worth a lot of money.

 ## She Says...

When the concept of this book came about, I told my co-authors that I believe the biggest difference between men and women during networking is the way that they use the VCP Process®. (Visibility, Credibility, and Profitability. Remember?) In my experience it seems that men move from the visibility phase of the relationship and go straight to the profitability phase, spending a very short period of time building the relationship in the credibility phase. Men tend to dive into the business part rather quickly.

On the other hand, women will move from the visibility phase of the relationship on to the credibility phase without ever evolving to the profitability phase, where referrals and business take place. I made this statement to Ivan and Frank based on my experience teaching and coaching people to build profitable networks. Both of them were of course a little hesitant to embrace the concept but very anxious to see if our data would prove it. It did, and we also received many comments in the same vein from our survey-takers:

> *When I meet with women to network and discuss business I find we spend about 90 percent of the time getting to know each other, discussing family, who we are, our backgrounds, etc., then we spend the remaining 10 percent of the time talking about business. When I meet with men we spend 10 percent of our time getting to know each other and 90 percent of our time talking about business. Both approaches are effective, but I enjoy networking with women more.*

> *I find that most women who network are definitely more interested in developing a relationship first and then business later. Most men get right into the part of the conversation where they ask what the other person does for work.*

> *In my experience, women tend to network intuitively, but tend to focus on relationship issues. Men tend to network by design, and tend to focus on business issues.*

Women want to take their time and get to know the people they're adding to their networks. It's not very often that I go into a networking event and have a woman I don't know start a conversation that within minutes turns into an attempt to transact business, be it a sale or a referral. I do have that happen with men fairly often. Not only have I experienced that repeatedly in business but also in my personal life. In the arena of dating or courtship, when men try to move from the visibility phase in a relationship to the profitability phase without even stopping to build a little credibility, it spells disaster.

Dating and business networking are more alike than different. They are both based on relationships that take time to create and require nurturing over time to be built in a way that is beneficial for both parties.

Finding myself in the single market, and loving to find new ways to network, I decided to try one of those online dating programs. After one particular gentleman (I use the term loosely here) and I had a few conversations, he asked me out on a date. I accepted and met him for a drink and a light meal, keeping it very casual, just the same as I would with meeting a fellow network member for the first time. Over the course of two hours and two glasses of wine we chatted in a breezy way about our families, professions, and hobbies.

I then decided to call it a night because I had to get up early the following morning. As we were heading towards the door, he put his arm around me and said, "How about you and I go out to the car and make out like teenagers?" I gave him the you-did-NOT-just-say-that glare, and told him, "No." I thought that was the end of it, and then he said, "Are you sure? It would be fun." I confirmed my answer and we called it a night. I've not heard from him since. He was racing toward profitability, when I hadn't even considered him for credibility yet. When a person rushes from visibility straight to profitability, they skip a lot of important graces, including manners. It's a premature solicitation, and that in the long run isn't good for either party. This survey respondent has witnessed the same thing:

> Women approach networking differently because to most of them, it is much more important to build a trusting relationship and then business just happens. With most men, they want to get right down to business and socialize after the deal is done. Women feel as though they are being coerced into a deal this way when all men are doing is getting the business out of the way so they can enjoy

the celebration and frankly will move on most of the time if they think there is any hesitation from you about business. This is just a communication problem. Men Are from Mars and Women Are from Venus comes to mind!

Building a strong network that supports both your personal and business goals requires time. There are no shortcuts to building relationships.

I see the very same scenario play out during business networking all the time. One of the biggest mistakes that networkers make is rushing relationships, much like my date did. It's not just men who do it, either. Occasionally I run into a go-getter female who wants to go immediately into either a sale or a referral relationship. Once this happens the connection is usually tainted without opportunity to correct it down the road. If it keeps happening, eventually that person develops an "avoid at all cost" reputation.

The Referral Institute has a unique five-step referral process. The first is the trust step, which takes the most time and cannot be rushed. The second is the knowledge step, during which you pass on the knowledge about your business. When I teach the steps there is inevitably a guy in the room who asks, "If I give you enough knowledge about me and my business it should establish trust. Right?" Wrong. Well, maybe not

PATTY AUBREY, PRESIDENT OF JACK CANFIELD INC.

It's easier to communicate with men. It's just information. It's simpler. Just get to the bottom line. For women—it's more emotional. You have to give them a story.

Women mix a little more personal into their business. Men tend to be more about business.

Women emotionally need more from a business relationship. Men are more to the point.

too wrong if the networking is between two men. But very wrong if the networking is between a man and woman. A guy's business acumen doesn't build trust with women, nor does it impress them. Women want to know about people, who they are, and what's personally important to them besides their businesses.

Guys, when you're working with the VCP Process®, you can't just jump from visibility to profitability in an hour. Learn from my unfortunate suitor!

The Way We Each Use the VCP Process®

Since the early 1990s, much research has been done on communication between the sexes by psychologists, biologists, and neuroscientists. It's clear that there are indeed brain differences between men and women that impact the way each prefers to communicate.

Women communicate from a place of emotion. They like to share the details of how, why, and where, as well as the feelings and emotions surrounding the information they convey.

When women are together, they go deep in conversations with one another, both in groups and one-on-one meetings. They communicate their experiences, sharing stories and collaborating for group consensus. The next time you have the opportunity to listen to a group of women, notice how they support and add to one another's stories and conversation themes.

I attended the first meeting of a new women's group one evening and was surprised how much personal information they shared with one another, having just met the other women in the group that night. I was also fascinated by how emotional they quickly became, revealing how they deeply felt about the things they talked about. It didn't take long for the conversation to swing around to men and how lacking they are in building up the personal elements of relationships.

Research states that women use twice as many words a day as men. We chat with our girlfriends and form deep relationships based on those chats. When we're having a conversation with someone, we're gauging the ability to connect and build trust and understanding.

SHE MEANS BUSINESS

Grant Schneider, author of *She Means Business: 7 New Rules for Marketing Today's Women*, had this to say about women and communication: "Women tend to communicate about most things, including products, in a storytelling style. This is distinctively a female form of communication and reflects the strong connection between women and their desire to help one another. In sharing stories, women recharge, learn, and form enduring bonds. Fewer men see the value in storytelling and are far less likely to view conversations as playing a critical role in their lives."

According to author John Gray,

When women are in a networking situation, they have a greater tendency to get to know people, and demonstrate that they are worthy of trust by showing interest and asking questions. Unfortunately, they're expecting the other person to reciprocate interest, which they may not always do. What women are not aware of is that what works with women does not always work with men.

When men are networking, their emphasis is on establishing who they are, what they've accomplished and achieved, what their responsibilities are, and what they can provide. They focus on how all of that can benefit others in terms of profitability, efficiency, and other benefits. Women don't end up having the opportunity to share what they have to offer and generate a business deal after all of that.

In other words, ladies, this is the point when we are often dismissed as not serious about our businesses. We fail to impress when we deviate to relational conversation, leaving the male to whom we are talking to believe that we are not serious.

3 / Communication: Transaction vs. Relationship

This is key information for women to understand when they network with men. Many women spend time trying to impress men with their sexuality, attire, and flirting, but men want to build credibility fast, and they want women to do the same. They want to know what women have achieved, what they're doing now, and how it can help them. In theory, this should work well in the networking world. Even though the advice wasn't intended for the dating arena, I may just give it a shot the next time I meet a guy who sparks my interest.

This is the very reason women feel networking is too sales-y and men feel that women don't take their businesses seriously. We come at this communication from two completely different motives. When women are communicating, they're trying to build a relationship of trust, and what the guy hears is a bunch of stuff he's not that interested in. So, ladies, let's try spending a little time impressing with our credentials "man style" and then hone in on the relationship-building questions. This quote from a survey respondent sums it up very well:

> *Generally speaking, I find that men are a lot more "in your face" when it comes to networking. Women often talk about everything but the business when you first meet—like movies, restaurants, and family. Then we talk about business. Men tend to get to the purpose of the conversation faster. This possibly helps make their conversations shorter, but I'm not sure that it fosters trust or strong relationships as much. The men I like to refer business to tend to be chatty, friendly men, because I feel I know them better.*

We must learn to use the VCP Process® effectively on both sides of the fence. Have you danced awkwardly with someone because you're both trying to lead? Whether it's the two-step or the cha-cha, both of you will fail if you mow down the other's moves. Yes, I know. That's the way most men dance anyway, but you know what I mean, ladies.

Both of us have to be dancing our complimentary roles in the same dance for things to work. Ladies, you are not going to be seen as serious about your business if you can't tell men about your accomplishments and goals and how that will help them. You've got to be able to brag up your own credibility. The biggest complaint I get from women is that networking with men is too sales-y. Maybe the real problem is that we're just not saying what they want to hear. If they want a two-step and we want a cha-cha, there are going to be some bruised shins.

Men, you can't impress women by dominating the conversation with what you've done and what you'll do for them. That's not even a conversation.

COURTESY OF *MERRIAM-WEBSTER*

con·ver·sa·tion *noun* \ ˌkänvər'sā sʜ ən \

An oral exchange of sentiments, observations, opinions, or ideas.

Notice the words "sentiments" and "exchange" in *Merriam-Webster's* definition of "conversation"? It's a back-and-forth process, fellas! Women are impressed when you reach out in an effort to get to know them and build trust with them. Doing the two-step is fun, but maybe it's time to add a new dance to your repertoire.

Having Clear Expectations and Communicating Your Needs

OK, we are about to go into sticky territory. We women think we communicate clearly with you men, but somehow, it gets all jumbled up once it hits your eardrums and brain. Men accuse women of not being direct about what they want or need, feeling like they have to be mind readers. Men rank very low on our gender quotient (GQ) scale at 1.74 while women come in much higher at 4.00.

Here's some fascinating information about GQ. Over millions of years, the sexes have been trying to understand one another. Books, movies, blogs, articles, studies, radio and TV shows have all been brought to the table in an attempt to teach the sexes to communicate with each other, with not much success. You'd think we'd understand one another after all of that. If that were the case, I would not be working on this book.

Here are few things that the gentlemen need to know in order to be successful networking with women:

- Stop trying to impress us quickly. We're impressed when you slow down enough to build a relationship of trust. I realize that in prehistoric times the strongest caveman won the rights to breed with women by bravado, but you're not that guy anymore, and we're pretty well past thinking being dragged by our hair into a cave is a good thing.
- Keep eye contact going when we're talking instead of looking over our shoulders or at our breasts.
- Our name badges are for knowing our names and not a one-way ticket to Gawkville.
- "Uh-huh" is not active listening, and we know it means you just want us to think you're listening.

OK. The list could go on forever, but you get the idea.

Ladies, when it comes to the GQ tally, women score higher because men are really pretty simple. Unfortunately, in business we often forget this, but it's a great clue that can help guide us in our communications with them.

Men are willing to ask for referrals before we are because they define relationships differently than we do. Just like my bad date, who was very clear with me about what he wanted me to do, men in business situations also want to get the business or referral volley going with you. There's no mystery about what a guy wants when he's in this mode. I appreciate that clear communication, which quickly presents the motive and gives me the opportunity to say yes or no and move on, just like with my date. It saved us both time once we had clearly communicated our desires.

Being clear about our expectations is the keystone of a strong referral relationship. Yet women are often reluctant to tell others what they want and expect. Don't get me wrong. I am not encouraging you to be like my date, at full speed to profitability in an hour. But we women do need to get clear with our networking partners about what we want from the business relationship. Instead of sitting back and only building, building, building, we have to do some self-searching and understand why we're building the relationship. What exactly do we want from our networking partner? How can they give it to us if we aren't clear on what it is ourselves and don't let them know what it is?

I teach a Certified Networker program for the Referral Institute. "Fifteen Ways Others Can Help You" is a section of the program in which the participants first create a list of tactics that will help their businesses and then ask their referral partners to help them with those items. I always get resistance from my female clients with this part of the program, explaining that they're not comfortable asking others to do those things for them. When I ask if they would be willing to do those things for their referral partners, I get a resounding "Yes!"

Why is it that they would have no problem at all doing any of the 15 items for another person, but can't turn the tables to help themselves? One of the reasons for the discomfort is that though they'd be happy to do those favors for someone, they're not comfortable asking that person to reciprocate. Neither do they want to impose on anyone, which makes complete sense when you consider that women are caretakers.

This is the same thing that happens at home. There can be piles of laundry on the kitchen table for hours that need to be taken upstairs and put away. I pass through the kitchen over and over and see that no matter how much time goes by, there they sit. There are a lot of people in the house who could put them away, but they all seem busy and it seems easier to just do it myself than take the time to relay the message to get it done.

Now I am aggravated. Why am I doing it all? There's no reason I should have to do all the housework! My husband and I are equally busy with full-time jobs and all kinds of obligations. When he gets wind of my irritation and asks what's wrong, I reply, "With all that laundry sitting there that you've passed twice as you've walked by, I don't understand why you haven't picked it up!" He replies, "You didn't ask me to." My retort to that is, "I shouldn't have to. You should have known that you're supposed to pick it up and just do it. Why do I always have to ask?"

Does this sound familiar? Of course it does. If we don't express our expectations clearly, others can't help us and we're left to do it all alone. This is not an effective way to build or run a business. For years I was superwoman and did it all, never asking for help. I left everyone around me guessing what I wanted and needed, not to mention how I did it all. I came to realize that my success was limited by my ability to do it all. If I was going to build a successful business or life, I was going to have to learn to be clear with others about my needs and expectations. We also must be willing to allow others to help us once we ask.

I listen to women complain all the time about how they have no work and personal life balance and have to do it all. When I ask if they've considered delegating some of the work at home to the spouse or kids I get the usual, "Oh, it is just easier if I do it myself." Really? Is that actually true? If it's so much easier, then why do they spend so much time moaning and complaining about it?

When I ask men why they don't help more, they say, "She doesn't ask, and when I do something for her, she's critical, saying that I didn't do it the way she would have." Ladies, all of this plays out the same way with the men in your network. You have to tell them what you want and need, be willing to delegate responsibility, and once you do that, let it go! If you want their business or a referral, then ask for it. Clear, direct, and simple (but polite) communication is the way to go with men in every area of life.

Men become confused and scared when trying to figure out what women want. They would rather stand in the middle of a football field with no pads on and let a 300-pound linebacker knock them to the ground than try to guess what we want, only to get it wrong.

Men and Shopping

Men approach shopping for themselves and with the woman in their lives much the same way they approach networking activities. They are direct, to the point, get what they want, and move on, but when they are standing across from a woman talking about personal stuff, their minds begin to wander.

Men don't browse and wander. They have a target, make a plan, and go and get the goal. How many men do you know who LIKE to shop? I mean for clothes and necessities for themselves. Few men that I have met actually enjoy the process of shopping for clothes. Some men even draw a map of the mall and then plan out their path from one store to the next, so they can be as efficient as possible. On that topic, I am thinking of coming up with an app called Mall GPS for Men that will allow men to map their way through the stores they need to go to using minimal time and effort.

I use to think that shopping was a learned behavior, but my son hated to be in the mall from the moment of birth. Every single time we went into the mall, he began to cry, later to beg, "Can we please go home now?"

The only thing men hate more than shopping for their own clothes is shopping with a woman for her clothes. Not only do they dislike shopping with women, but when they're shopping with us they're actually thinking of ways to injure themselves, just to be excused from the activity.

How do I know this? I was torturing one man to give me the "inside scoop" on how men think, and after three days of unending questions, got him to reveal the universal male thought process on mall shopping with women. Incidentally, this secret source of male mall anguish is my co-author Frank!

He Comments . . .

Yes, as soon as we pull into the giant mall parking lot, the survival flight instinct kicks in with ideas for feigning injury. What if I pretended to trip? I could fall down, say I hurt my knee, and we would have to go home. I could also go into the bathroom and say I got sick. No, wait! I could slam myself against the wall and the urinals and say I was mugged. That could work. Better yet, I know what I can do. I can close a door on my fingers. Sure, it might hurt for a little bit but it would be worth it. Wait a minute. I got it! If I jump from this second floor balcony to the first floor of the mall I could break my leg and that one would get me out of coming to the mall with her for at least eight weeks! Very cool. But if I hit my head when I land and get a concussion it would buy me 10 or 12 weeks! That's the ticket. It's worth it to put an end to this torture of store to store, blouse to blouse, shoe to shoe. Here I goooooo!

"FRANK!"

"Huh, what, honey? Oh, yes, those shoes go perfectly with your peach blouse and pant set." Just shoot me now!

Of course most, if not all, men will completely deny this when you ask them.

She Responds . . .

The point is, men are comfortable being direct, just doing things to get them done, and once they have completed the task at hand, they are then completely open to relating. Women are less comfortable with a direct approach. It does not mean either of us is wrong, but we can both adjust. It's a matter of what route we each choose to take, as expressed here:

Men seem to start talking business right away, whereas women seem to start on a more personal level. For example, a man's first question to me is usually, "So, what do you do?" A woman's first question is usually something like, "So, how did you find out about our organization?"

Building credibility and profitability with members in our network means we have to learn to communicate effectively, not just in the way we want to be communicated with, but the way our conversation partner wants to be communicated with. For instance, if I'm at a networking event and meet a gentleman for the first time, it's important for me to understand that he's likely to try and impress me and want me to impress him. After that's done, we can move to building trust and credibility. Once he knows I am serious about my business and helping others, I can move toward building a more personal relationship with him.

CHERYL BAKER, CEO OF HUMAX

So many times, men would make the business request really clearly and obviously, pretty much inside our SMART description of specific, meaningful, authentic, relevant, and timely. What would happen is sometimes women would do one of two things. They would make a request for a greater good, rather than a specific business need to be met. The activity could help at a moral or value-based level for a personal cause, and they would put their cause forward in their request, rather than meeting business needs.

An example would be they have a specific job at this location and they are on the board for a homeless shelter. We'd find that they'd often put forward the need of the homeless shelter rather than trying to help themselves in their job.

The Survey Says...
Business vs. Relationship by Success

We looked at the responses from people who said that networking had in fact played a role in their success, and within that group we compared those who said they focus first on business with those who said they first focus on the relationship. We discovered that 87.1 percent of the people who said that networking had played a role in their success also felt that it was better to build a relationship first and then focus on the business!

An emphasis on relationships first was clearly and undeniably a key factor in determining whether people were going to identify with networking as having played a role in their success. People who feel that networking has played a role in their success tend to focus on building the relationship before conducting business. This seems to point out the efficacy of the relationship-first approach.

Those who skip the relationship building and attempt to establish an "all business" interaction often discover that trust and goodwill are more than just window dressing—they are part of the social capital that energizes a mutually rewarding business relationship. People who bypass relationship building are more likely to feel that networking has not contributed to their success, and they are probably right—because they're doing it wrong. The networking relationships that grow out of the VCP Process® are far stronger, more durable, and more profitable than the impersonal, business-only arrangements that some think of as networking.

If your networking efforts focus on the transaction and not the relationship, the data seems to indicate very clearly that you will not be nearly as satisfied with your success in the process. In other words, you're much more likely to feel that networking has played a role in your success if you focus on building the relationship first and then focusing on the business.

Interestingly, our survey data shows that women seem to do a bit better in this area than men. Not only do women tend to have a relational focus, but you'll see later in the book how this has an effect on the percentage of business that women generate compared to men.

Gender aside, though, here's the take-away lesson that we think is pretty, well, sexy: Networkers who focus primarily on relationships are more successful.

♂ He Says . . .

We just want to get things done. We take the quickest route possible to get what we need done in the most efficient way. For us, business isn't about the relationship until after the deal is done. We talk business, do the deal, then build the relationship with our customers, clients, and the person who gave us the referral. If I believe that the person before me is credible, can do what he says, and will make me look good if I give him business or referrals, then and only then am I really interested in the relationship.

Doing the business first is how we build the relationship with others. After that we can go out for a drink, play golf, and connect more deeply.

When networking with women, this approach does not work. Women want to know us, like us, and trust us before they give us business or refer us to those people in their networks.

Men, ladies are top-notch at getting and giving referrals. When we do not take the time to build the relationship, or take them seriously, we lose in a big way. It won't hurt us to slow down, listen, and get to know our female fellow networkers. Instead of jumping from visibility straight to profitability, we should slow down for the credibility phase of the relationship and build stronger, more effective relationships.

PREMATURE SOLICITATION
BY IVAN MISNER

Has someone you didn't even know ever solicited you for a referral or business? I call this "Premature Solicitation." (Say that fast three times and you might get in trouble!)

I've been a victim of "premature solicitation" many times. I was recently speaking at a business networking event, and, before my presentation, a man came up to me and said, "Hi, it is a real pleasure to meet you. I understand you know Richard Branson. I offer specialized marketing services and I am sure his Virgin enterprises could benefit from what I provide. Could you please introduce me to him so that I can show him how this would assist his companies?"

OK, so what I was thinking was:

Are you completely insane? I'm going to introduce you, someone I don't know and don't have any relationship with, to Sir Richard, whom I've only met a few times, so that you can proceed to attempt to sell him a product or service that I don't know anything about and haven't used myself? Yeah, right. That's NEVER going to happen.

I am pleased to report, however, that with much effort, I was able to keep that little monologue inside my own head, opting instead for a much more subtle response.

PREMATURE SOLICITATION, CONTINUED

I replied, "Hi, I'm Ivan, I'm sorry—I don't think we've met before, what was your name again?" That surprised the man enough to make him realize that his "solicitation" might have been a bit "premature." I explained that I regularly refer people to my contacts, but only after I've established a long-term, strong relationship with the service provider first. He said thanks and moved on to his next victim.

What was even more amazing to me was that a few months later I blogged about my experience on one of my favorite online social networks. A great dialogue ensued with most people sharing their horror stories and frustrations about people who pounce on them at networking meetings asking for business even though they've never met the person before.

Every time I start to think this is an almost universal feeling of distaste for that approach to networking, I am brought back to reality by the minority of people who still think that this is actually a good networking technique.

To my astonishment, a man on the forum actually wrote:

> I don't happen to believe that you need a relationship with the person you are asking first. What you must have is a compelling story or product/service that would genuinely benefit the referral. The fact that you had not cultivated a relationship with the person has become irrelevant because, more importantly, you had been in a position to help [your contact] benefit from the introduction. If it's of genuine benefit to the person being referred, I don't see the problem.

> It's about the benefit of what's being referred rather than the relationship with the person asking for the referral.

> Who am I to deny my contacts something good?

Wow. What can I say? The "relationship" is irrelevant! All you have to have is a good story, product, or service and I owe it to you or any stranger (who says he or she has a good product) to introduce him or her to a good contact of mine! Really? People really think

PREMATURE SOLICITATION, CONTINUED

this way!? According to this writer, it doesn't matter if I actually know or trust the person wanting the business. As long as the person has a good product (or so he says), I should refer that person because I would otherwise "deny" my contacts "something good"!

Networking is not about hunting. It is about farming. It's about cultivating relationships. Don't engage in "premature solicitation." You'll be a better networker if you remember that.

 She Says . . .

Of course the relationship is the most important thing. We have been saying that since the days of planned marriages between kingdoms. "But Mom, I really want to love the man I marry. I don't want it to be a business merger." It is always about the relationship first, but it cannot be only about the relationship. We have to strike that happy balance, creating a relationship that we can turn to and ask for business referrals or connections. When we are in a good relationship with our network members, they are more than happy to make the connections for us.

4

Gender-Specific Networking Obstacles

The Survey Says...
Best Time to Network

Having run the world's largest networking organization for many years, I occasionally hear people express concern about family obligations interfering with their ability to attend business meetings. I went into this survey expecting to see a dramatic difference between men and women on this issue. What I saw surprised me.

Many women told me that attending networking meetings in the morning was very hard for them. This is understandable, because even though our society is more gender-equal than in the past, a large number of women have told me that the lion's share of household operation, organizing family events, and taking kids to school are still handled by women. Yet in our survey results, the difference between men and women turned out to be very small; only a few more women (9.3 percent) than men (8.4 percent) expressed difficulty with morning meetings. Almost 22 percent of men, compared with about 19 percent of women, said that it was always easier to attend networking functions in the morning. Although the women in our survey found morning meetings to be less convenient, it was not by a large factor.

This may be another example of the exception becoming the perception—the perception in this case being my own. The women who emotionally vented their dissatisfaction with morning meetings seemed like a larger group than they actually were. This poses the question of to what degree do emotionally relayed messages affect our perception of facts, as well as our tendency to remember bad news or negative stereotypes?

EMOTION OR FACT?

If a listener receives the same message first from a nonemotive speaker, merely relaying the facts, and then from an emotional, distressed speaker, the listener is more likely to dramatize or magnify the information received from the second scenario. The flip side of the dramatic, emotional delivery of a message is that the listener may actually discount the information, thinking it is exaggerated. Think of the classic scenario that most of us have been through, in which an acquaintance known for theatrics emotionally relays a dramatic message. Do you doubt that the scene they describe is not enhanced just a little bit? Heightened emotion usually transfers from speaker to listener, and is a technique most great speakers have finessed to an art form because of its power to manipulate.

Having been told directly by a few women that it might be a problem, I immediately became concerned that by scheduling meetings in the morning we might be causing difficulty for most women in the organization, perhaps unintentionally causing them to leave our group. As it turned out, the problem was not widespread, and without complaint, the women throughout the organization attended morning meetings with the same regularity and commitment as the men. Being sensitive to gender-related problems caused me to see the potential morning meeting problem as larger and more worrisome than it actually was. This is another example of how emotion attached to fact can magnify perception.

Despite the fact that the data doesn't show a substantial difference between men and women on this issue, the few women who disapprove of morning meetings seem to be very strongly against them. Notice the woman's choice of words in the irate feedback below.

My parenting responsibilities make an early breakfast time impossible. Women are unable to participate in morning meetings because they have chosen to be great parents, too. That's just a sad day for a networking group! I've often wondered if the misogynistic jerks who run these groups will ever figure out that women control more spending than men do, are better networkers, and responsible for more small-business startups than men are. Their loss.

Ladies, please don't shoot the messenger: The data doesn't show a big difference between the way men and women feel about the time of day networking meetings occur. The comments certainly do, though. This indicates that although there is not a big difference in the number of survey responses on each side, there is a pretty high level of intense feeling attached to the subject in those who felt negatively about it.

A number of women expressed concern about the meeting time being a challenge for other women, as well as some men, as you'll see in the comment below:

I have heard several times that women generally find early morning networking more difficult to attend as they are usually the ones doing the child minding, taking the children to school, etc.

In light of those few responses disapproving of morning meetings, it appears overall that it didn't matter a great deal to either gender whether the meetings were held in the morning, at noon, or in the evening, even though women found family obligations to be a bit more of an obstacle to networking than did men.

Although the degree of the problem does not appear to be as big as the expressive vocalization may make it seem, my perception is that it is a serious problem for some individuals.

Networking at lunch was preferred more strongly by women, at twice the response rate (8.7 percent) as men (4.7 percent), agreeing that it was always a better time. Men and women rated networking in the evening virtually the same.

♂ He Says . . .
The Benefits of Networking Outweigh Scheduling Obstacles

I hear people talk about networking events as obligations, which I don't understand. How are meeting, schmoozing, and socializing as a low-cost, high-benefit tool for getting business a pain in the rear? People talk about it like it's a chore. If I have a choice of marketing my business by spending lots of money on advertising for the hopes of a significant return on my investment or spending a lot less on advertising by networking with those in my local community, it is a NO-BRAINER, especially since the lasting effects of business gained by networking are more solid than those of paid advertising!

The message I'm about to give is really for men, but should be considered by women, too. Spending money needlessly on marketing is just stupid. The benefits of face-to-face networking not only outweigh paid advertising, but stretch far beyond just growing your business. Guys, if you persist in discounting networking and some of the small challenges that accompany it, you're foolish!

First, let's take a hard look at financial benefits. As you know, in any business there are both soft- and hard-money costs to consider. "Hard money" is that which you take out of your pocket and includes credit cards, cash, checks, and other possessions with monetary value. The term "soft money" is used to assign value to services or invested time, otherwise known as sweat equity. It's not a tangible financial extraction from your bank account or pocket; rather, it's your very valuable time. People tend to invest larger dollar amounts in the form of sweat equity or soft money than they may want to spend in actual greenbacks, dough, clams, or Benjamins. Catch my drift? The riches that invested time reaps are greater than hard money spent. You also get more value for your soft-money investments than you would for spending what you think the equivalent is in moolah.

If you were to add up the soft-money investments of labor, networking, connecting, and building relationships you may be surprised at the financial value you've delivered to your business.

Wait a minute. Does that contradict networking being a no-brainer that saves us money because we are "spending" more soft money? Absolutely not, because when networking is practiced effectively, especially for the small-business owner and sales professional, it yields richer, more lasting results than just advertising.

Let's look at the array of positive wealth effects that networking brings, beyond just sales numbers.

- Added sales volume
- Higher average transaction amount per sale
- Greater closing ratio
- Referrals tend to be very qualified professionals
- Higher occurrences of leads and referrals
- More repeat business
- Greater positive word-of-mouth marketing benefits
- More customer loyalty
- Stronger community recognition
- Greater perceived value

The more solid relationships you build, the more credible you are. The more your credibility grows, the more people will hire and recommend you. The impression of quality is created through networking. By the validation of many people vouching for you, your name is passed along with more and more frequency and confidence. After you have repeatedly established proof of quality, you'll be referred in such a manner that neither your rates nor quality are questioned.

ILLUMINATE YOUR QUALITY AND ETHICS

The impression of quality is a powerful one. It is well-known that consumers are willing to pay more for services and products that they equate to be high in both ethical and product value. From locally grown organic produce and safer foods to fair-trade-produced coffee and businesses that donate a portion of their proceeds to philanthropic ventures, consumers, by their spending choices, are showing the market that ethics and quality are what they want. What better way to convey the image of quality for your business than with the vote of those who believe in you so much that they can't stop talking about you?

Advertising is a powerful and important asset to a business, but cannot replace the credibility and reputation that is built by physical, social interaction, which can enhance your reputation and create a higher awareness of your credibility. If you present yourself and your service shiningly, it can also spread the reputation of your goodwill, intelligence, friendliness, and good deeds like wildfire. People want to do business with people, not companies or figureheads. For a business catering to the local consumer, the most important marketing they can invest in is getting out and networking effectively in their immediate area.

As a man, I prefer morning meetings because they don't create as much of an interruption in my nine-to-five workday as other time slots do. Of course it's easier to go to a meeting before or after work, but obstacles aside, in the end, I will do what it takes! When one realizes the enormous value gained from networking, the inconvenience of adjusting schedules to get to meetings doesn't merit complaining.

I'd rather not stop my workday to go to a lunchtime meeting, and at the end of the day I'm tired and would prefer to go home and relax with my family, but if there is a networking opportunity that has value to me, I'll go. Why? Because I'm the hunter! It's my job to hunt down money and bring it home to my family. That's my unwavering responsibility, and the more often I'm seen (visibility), the more people will remember me. The deeper my relationships become because of my tending to them, the more solid my reputation (credibility) becomes.

Please understand that I'm not denying the value or importance of advertising. On the contrary, if you're networking and becoming well-known, an appropriately timed, strategic advertising or marketing plan can build your brand credibility with speed and strength. The key thing to remember is that people have to see you to know you exist. Your spark, integrity, and grit are what people will talk about, so you've got to be out shaking hands and kissing babies, as the saying goes, to show them how great you are.

⚥ She Says . . .

This statistic surprised me! Men and women were in agreement that their lunch hour was the best time slot for networking, preferring it over morning and evening. There also were larger than expected numbers of women who thought that morning and evening options were just fine. Surprise, surprise! I fully expected to find a large number of women opposed to those slots because of family obligations.

One of the most common complaints about getting to network meetings that I've heard from women over the course of my career as a BNI director is that they can't get to the morning ones because they have to get their kids to school and day care. Imagine my surprise to learn that the data did not prove this to be an accurate generalization of most women. I can only assume this is an excuse used by women who don't want to go to a meeting but have trouble saying "No." The next question revealed that neither women nor men felt that family obligations, for the most part, get in the way of their networking activities. That really compounded my surprise.

Do women use family obligations as a way of justifying not being active or joining groups? Is it possible that they may be just wriggling sideways out of invitations to avoid confrontation? Perhaps they have a hard time making statements like, "No, I just don't feel that this group would be a good fit for me." Whether or not this is true and to what degree isn't clear, but for you women who actually see scheduling as a big hurdle and feel time challenged, I have some ideas that may make it easier for you to balance business networking and family life.

- Develop systems around your networing activities that include tracking
- Choose the right type of networking activites
- Automate your network so you can spend time working your network instead of just networking

Too often we find ourselves running from one even to the next, with no real goal or plan or what we want to accomplish. Then we end up spending our time having the wrong conversations, with the wrong

FAMILY: AN EQUAL OPPORTUNITY ENDEAVOR

Greater numbers of men are taking on more family obligations as their spouses work. Guys! Guess what? That takes some of the income responsibility off your plate, delegates some of that workload to women, allows them to share that responsibility, and creates adjustments that will benefit you.

people at the wrong time. The above three tips will help create more balance because you will have more clear focus.

Of course you need to network during times that balance managing a household and your family life. Additional hurdles are if your employment hours are late at night and you can't get to early morning breakfast meetings, or if your job starts very early and there's no room for flexibility or understanding from your employer on an occasional later start time. You may want to broach the subject with your boss to see if it's even an option.

Additionally, if your workday really gets hopping midafternoon, frenetic with client meetings or trips across town, you may want to avoid networking lunch meetings because you might have a hard time getting there in a timely manner.

Choose what works in harmony with your lifestyle and schedule. Evening may be your quality family or social time, so committing to evening meeting groups, even if you could get to some of them, could cause stress and challenges for you in the long run. Remember that you have to be involved with the group in a committed way over time if you expect to get optimum results. That means the time you budget toward the organization isn't just dedicated to the typical meetings.

Allow room in your schedule so that you may also donate time to sub-committees within the group or volunteer to coordinate or lead projects and possibly come early and stay late for meetings. All of these details are the labor of love you invest in the organization, and ultimately, your business. All too often people join groups when they really don't have the time to remain actively involved with them in a quality way. It's better to belong to fewer groups that you can really invest in than lots of groups that you wind up not showing up for or only shallowly participating in. You'll just get frustrated by lack of results if you don't choose the former, not to mention that the organization will miss out on any benefits your deeper participation would have brought to the table, had you focused on quality, rather than quantity.

The Survey Says ...
Family Obligations

Although family obligations were not a big issue to most, Figure 4.1 shows that women generally found it to be a problem slightly more than did men; 37 percent of our women respondents said sometimes to always (25.1 percent plus 11.9 percent combined), compared with 32.8 percent (23.2 percent plus 9.6 percent) of men for the same categories. This is not a huge difference, but it is statistically significant.

Statement to rate: I find that family obligations prevent or hinder me from networking.		
	Female	**Male**
Usually or always	11.9%	9.6%
	(663)	(531)
Sometimes	25%	23.2%
	(1,394)	(1,285)
Never or rarely	63%	67.2%
	(3,502)	(3,719)

FIGURE 4.1—**Family Obligations by Gender**

One female respondent added:

Networking events are attended by fewer women because they have family commitments.

Another woman said:

Women tend to network less due to family obligations, especially those with young children.

Again, the degree of the problem does not appear to match the vocalization of the problem. Though these responses indicate women found family obligations to be slightly more of an obstacle to networking

WHAT'S THE MATTER?

Why is each gender troubled with its own unique obstacles to networking? From family responsibilities to other scheduling challenges such as lack of motivation or problems being assertive, women have a gamut of preoccupations that act as obstacles to networking. Men seem to have more trouble with social mores and practicing sensitivity in the networking process.

A fascinating study by psychology professor Richard Haier of the University of California, Irvine, in conjunction with colleagues from the University of New Mexico, delves into the matter of matter—that is, the gray and white matter that make up our brain tissue. Though it is known that both sexes score equally in general intelligence tests, new information from this study gives the mystery about intelligence types more clarity. Their study revealed that men have almost 6.5 times more gray matter related to general intelligence. Women have almost 10 times the amount of white matter related to intelligence.

Gray matter's primary function is to process information and white matter's is to integrate, network, and distribute the information harvested from the gray matter. Another point worth noting is that the gray matter in women's brains is distributed more within the white matter, rather than as it is in men's brains— more separated. This explains why women excel in language, communal activities, and connecting, where men are more goal-, mathematics-, and task-driven.

than did men, the survey reflects that family obligations don't represent a substantially larger challenge for them than their male counterparts.

♂ He Says...
The Conflict Between Family Obligations and Networking

As the breadwinner, my primary responsibility to my family is to provide. I must provide a dwelling, food, heat, transportation, and all the other stuff that costs money. Though female primary breadwinners are on the rise, in more than 60 percent of households, men still hold that role, with the women being the primary caretaker of the family, according to a WorkingMother.com survey done in 2010.

The responsibilities of caretaker and breadwinner alike are not easy, and the hours of sweat equity invested are many. The duties and requirements cost money, energy, and most importantly, time. For the breadwinner, that time spent is usually away from family. It's unfortunate, but I must do what I must do to provide for my family and maintain the lifestyle that my wife and I have decided is right for us.

Networking is an important part of my business. Building relationships, creating visibility, and taking advantage of introduction opportunities to new professionals in the community are all mandatory aspects to growing a local business. Does family time suffer because of it? Regrettably, yes.

I'd like women reading this to understand that for most men, time away from family is not what we want. It is simply what must be done. The reason family time does not get in the way of my networking is because I know that in order for my family to remain my primary commitment, focusing on my business must remain my primary objective.

There are cycles in which I produce the necessary cash flow to meet the family goals, and then I can relax, or "coast" for a little bit and spend time with the family, but then the cycle inevitably starts up again and I have to honor the ebb and flow of keeping the bank ledger balanced. Also, by working extra hard on nights and mornings that aren't reserved for important family events, I can get a little ahead and then be free to enjoy time with my family.

♀ She Says . . .

It's 4:00 P.M. and I've worked a long day, starting with getting the family and myself out the door early in the morning, to shuttle each of us to our respective activities. In the span of a typical day, the speed of duties is breakneck. I'm running one child to soccer and another to baseball, picking up the dry cleaning, rushing home to get the kids started on their homework for school tomorrow, doing a couple of loads of laundry, putting the dog out, answering the phone, and packing lunches for tomorrow. At the end of the day, while I'm still in the middle of all this, I hear a voice shouting through the house, straining over the din of the TV, that asks, "Honey, what's for dinner?" I stop in my tracks and think, What is wrong with him? It's like having one more child in the house.

As a mom, wife, and business owner, managing my time is extremely important. I'm always seeking some sort of balance between those three areas. Most of the time, I feel like the ringmaster of a three-ring circus with lots of out-of-control clowns running around me. Before I learned the delicate balancing act of time management, I knew that networking was important for creating visibility for my business, but was torn between commitments with my kids, spouse, school participation, and PTA involvement.

If I was going to a networking event, I had to make sure family was cared for in my absence. If it was an evening meeting, and I left the kids with Dad, I had to make sure he had something ready to feed them and leave notes reminding them to get their homework done. When I got home from the meeting tired, I still had to make sure their breakfast and lunch money were set out and ready to go for the next morning. Time permitting, I might even be lucky enough to throw in a load of laundry before bed. This chaos and over-demand can be overwhelming and probably is the reason so many women choose to network less than their male counterparts.

The biggest complaint I hear from women is their inability to attend networking events because of family issues such as getting kids to school or day care. In my own experience it made it difficult for me to network at times. There are more networking opportunities today than there were in the early 1990s, so women now may have a wider variety of choices to accommodate their family schedules.

The very fact that we are so busy being the ringmasters of our own personal circuses makes it vitally important to make the best use of our networking and business time allotments. Both genders can help

WHO'S RUNNING THE HOUSE?

Networking events take place every day of the week, and in many different time frames from early mornings and lunch hours to evenings. Finding the right way to make it all fit together can be a bit of a challenge. An article titled "Battle of the Sexes" by MySalary.com shows how men and women divvy their time among life's responsibilities. The statistical data is from the American Time Use Survey, courtesy of the Bureau of Labor Statistics.

1. *Full-time workers*: Men averaged 8.2 hours daily, which was slightly longer than women, who averaged 7.8.
2. *Chores*: On an average day, 20 percent of men did housework such as cleaning or laundry, compared to 52 percent of women.
3. *Meals*: Thirty-seven percent of men did food prep or cleanup compared with 64 percent of women. If this indicates men were otherwise occupied during cleanup by the eating part of the equation, would anyone really be surprised?
4. *Child care*: During the average weekday, women spent 1.2 hours providing physical child care such as bathing or feeding, while men spent 23 minutes. On weekends, women provided about an hour of physical care to household children and men spent about half an hour.

A recent U.S. Census Bureau survey counts approximately 13.7 million single parents in the United States. Eighty-four percent of them are moms, and the remaining 16 percent, fathers. This group will no doubt require more scheduling flexibility and time management skills to allow them time for committed networking.

I can hear the ladies out there thinking, OK, now tell me something I didn't already know!

themselves by developing good networking habits, meaning spending lots of quality time building deeper connections with the networks they are already part of rather than running around trying to meet more new people. This can be done in a very manageable fashion and will glean rich results from invested time.

The Survey Says . . .
Safety

One area in which we might expect to find sex differences is in personal safety. Indeed, this question that unveiled one of the most dramatic differences between male and female views.

Participants were asked whether they felt unsafe attending networking events in the evening. Figure 4.2 shows how they responded.

Statement to rate: I feel unsafe attending networking events when they are in the evening.			
	Female	**Male**	
1) Never	63.6% (3,509)	82.4% (4,524)	
2)	19.2% (1,507)	8.4% (461)	
3)	10.7%	5.8%	
4)	4.6% (255)	1.7% (94)	
5) Always	1.9% (103)	1.8% (97)	
Rating average	1.62 (5,516)	1.32 (5,492)	1.47 (11,008)

FIGURE 4.2—**Safety by Gender**

This result seems to indicate a strong difference between the sexes at the "never" end of the scale, with considerably more men—more than 82 percent—saying they never felt unsafe attending evening events, and fewer than 64 percent of the women responding similarly. At the other extreme, although they numbered fewer than 7 percent, nearly twice as many women as men said they always or usually felt unsafe at evening events (the last two categories combined). Although these numbers reflect what one might expect, they are a bit surprising in light of the near-identical preferences expressed by men and women concerning evening meetings.

♂ He Says . . .
Lack of Safety at Networking Events

The survey respondents' comments below reveal yet another obstacle to networking: safety. Opposing motives and communication barriers between the genders create safety issues, and this time we really are talking about SEX!

> I am intimidated by men at networking events. I also do not want them to think I'm approaching them for inappropriate reasons.

> Perhaps the hardest thing about networking from a woman's point of view is that in many cases men assume that women who talk to them are interested in going to bed with them!

> As a woman, I think there is a fine line when networking with some men. They often think that you're interested in them other than on a business level and you have to cautiously balance levels of openness and friendliness with a high level of knowledge and professionalism to convince them you are capable.

> The only problem I have networking with the opposite sex is being hit on. This has happened to me on more occasions than I would like to remember. Due to some men's seemingly uncontrollable behavior, it has affected how I approach networking with men in general. Men, when networking, please remember that we are intelligent human beings. Don't degrade yourself and us by making it sexual. You'll lose the sale every time!

When attending more casual contact networking events, I sometimes get "creepy" vibes from some men. I get the feeling they are there for more than business networking.

These are only a few of many comments, but do I need to go on? It's hard to believe, but this kind of comment was the most common type we received. Guys, is this really necessary? Are you really that desperate? Talk about building a reputation! If this is how you're acting, you certainly are building a reputation, and trust me, it's not helping you, and I doubt it's the kind of reputation you want. This is why women are scared to go to evening networking events. I can't even tell you how embarrassing this is to me as a man. I can't think of a better example of the exception becoming the perception. It hurts all of us.

I am sure you can guess that very few men felt uncomfortable attending networking events, no matter what time of day. The funny part is that women who said they felt unsafe were fearful of the men in the networking events and not the ones that may be lurking outside in the parking lot. Women were afraid of unprofessional and inappropriate behavior from men; in other words: being hit on, approached, talked to, or touched in a way that suggested or blatantly stated more than friendship was desired. Once again, to all women out there, on behalf of men everywhere, I apologize.

Men, are you kidding me? I mean, seriously! Do you realize you're acting like a college frat boy? Let me refer you back to the VCP principle. Do you think this builds your credibility? Business functions are for business, not for going after the new, hot chick. Okay, I know that not all of you do this, but remember that the exception creates the perception.

♀ She Says . . .
We Are Vulnerable

There are multiple things that might make a woman feel uncomfortable networking in the evening, especially if she is going to the event alone.

From car problems and muggings to any other problems that might put her at risk, women just feel more vulnerable when they're out at night alone. Are those fears realistic or just an exaggeration of the unknown? The nightly news and crime TV shows compound this fear by using the repetitive theme of women getting slain within all kinds of interchanging themes, when they are alone, and usually at night. If one woman is mugged or abducted in the area, all women will feel that sense of fear and be reminded of how vulnerable they are.

Men believe they can take care of themselves, and walking down a dimly lit street to a networking event is rarely an issue for them. Heck, they used to slay dinosaurs with sticks and stones, and fight battles with knives and swords. Why would they worry about lurking creeps?

Behavior changes at evening business networking events where the attitude is more relaxed and free-spirited, unlike the brighter, straight-edged tone at breakfast and lunch meetings. Men and women alike become more relaxed by having a few drinks in the evening. Unfortunately, some men and women drink more than they should and get a little too relaxed. Once too much booze has been consumed, people say and do things that are completely inappropriate, from making off-color comments all the way to inappropriate touching. Here are some examples of booze and business going sour in the eyes of our survey respondents:

> At many evening network meetings, there are cocktails involved and almost always one person, usually a male, who indulges a bit too much. Once that happens the networking turns into flirting. I've seen it devolve into downright "hitting on" female participants. I imagine that this is intimidating or irritating to some of them. On more than one occasion I've been embarrassed by that behavior if I'm in the conversation circle it happens in.

> When I first began my business, I joined the local chamber of commerce. Young, female, single, and naive, I frequently found myself in uncomfortable situations with men.

4 / Gender-Specific Networking Obstacles

I used to network with a lot of males during happy hours and dinners. However, 60 percent of the time I got the impression that it was about to turn into them hitting on me or taking it to an unprofessional level.

One of the biggest problems with the flirting confrontation is that many women just don't know what to do about it. They wind up just walking away because they don't want to cause trouble. Sometimes they even convince themselves that they just misinterpreted the bad behavior. I never cease to be amazed by the things that happen at networking events where there is free or cheap alcohol being served.

Do some guys look forward to these events because they intend to hit on women? I've certainly heard this more than once. Here are more comments from our survey that may make you wonder:

As a young woman I find the networking scene to be dominated by men of a certain age who enjoy a drink. This environment makes it hard to be taken seriously in. Whilst there is nothing wrong with this per se, I often also have men making inappropriate sexual advances, comments, and even make-believe business opportunities so that they can extend our conversations.

I have been in networking situations with men that resulted in uncomfortable banter generated from the other male participants in our conversation circle. They know I'm married with a child! What is up with that?

Come on, guys, networking events are not dating scenes. If you want to pick up women, join a dating network. If you're at a business event, then respectfully keep it professional. Do yourself a favor by showing genuine interest and respect. If the woman you are talking to is interested beyond that, you can get to know her over time, but fabricating fake business agendas and hitting on her will just ruin your credibility and generate negative word-of-mouth. It also creates the perception that men hit on women all the time; another exception that creates a perception.

Here are some more quotes on that experience:

As a naive businesswoman I wasted a lot of time talking to men who PRETENDED to be seriously interested in my business and developing a professional business relationship. They would show their true intentions (sex) by the end of the event or at a lunch appointment. It took a long time for me to learn how to separate the serious male professional from the man on the make.

I notice that men tend to flirt more, especially if the female is young, attractive, and I hate to say this . . . blonde. That's been my observation. I also notice that men give women more attention based on the "lack" of business attire they may be wearing.

Ladies, when a man at a business event treats you inappropriately, speak up right away and let him know that what he said was not appreciated or acceptable. You don't have to scream and shout. You can be professional while at the same time letting him know you do not condone or expect such behavior from him or others. Keeping quiet and walking away allows this kind of man to victimize others and actually leaves him with the idea that you were OK with his advances.

Every time you fail to speak up, you leave more bad behavior for other women to have to deal with in the future. If we collectively give the message that this is not acceptable, then the behavior should disappear over time because these men will cease to get rewards from it. People only do what keeps working for them or that which gives them some kind of reward.

Alternate Perceptions, Differing Preferences

The Survey Says . . .
Preferences for Different Types of Networking Events

We found more evidence of differing preferences between the sexes when we asked people what kind of networking events they liked. In general, women were more flexible about networking than men, who were more likely to specify either structured or unstructured events. In addition, males expressed a stronger preference than women for structured events (such as referral networking groups).

Brain differences between the genders might help explain what appears to be a more holistic approach to networking by women versus a narrower, structured approach by many men. Plenty of female respondents complained about what they saw as a ham-handed, "what's in it for me?" manner of networking by some men. This respondent's observations reflect a facet of that difference:

Within my network, I find that the women are more skilled at asking me about what I do and need, as well as talking about what they do and need. Some of the men seem to have little skill in building information and real connection outside of their own field of work.

Other respondents' comments, however, suggested that the combination of the male and female styles makes for a more balanced and satisfying networking experience. This respondent acknowledges the differences—but sees benefits in men and women working in tandem to enrich the process and value of networking:

Though there are many differences between the networking styles of men and women, I've found in my six years of business that it is the mix and complement of each style that makes the networking events successful.

Beyond just noting the balancing effect of mixing both genders' networking styles, some of our respondents actually craved it, as mentioned in this observation on an unbalanced, all-female group:

After attending a new women's networking group, I felt hollow, unproductive, and robbed of my time. As a woman business owner of a women's health service, I was hoping to gain perspective on other women's experiences. However, what I walked into was a sappy, emotional, territorial meeting where one woman shared her most recent challenge and the other women told her how they would have done it their way, not how she could have learned from the experience. I truly believe that even though men and women have preferences and tendencies when it comes to networking and business, it is the complement and the synergy between the two which makes entrepreneurs and business growth successful.

Does the presence of the opposite sex apply pressure to both sexes to be on more formal, or at least better, behavior? Is there such a thing as feeling too comfortable at meetings where everyone is alike? The comment below seems almost inspired by mixed groups:

I find the healthiest networking groups tend to have a fairly equal mix of men and women as members. There is a certain richness of experience to be had when there is a good mix of the two genders, which doesn't exist to the same degree when it's only one or the other in the room. Each gender brings different gifts and perspectives to the table, and by leveraging the skills and characteristics of both men and women, the success of the team can be taken to new heights.

As a woman, I have on occasion visited women's networking organizations and have found that rather than being positive and productive, those groups I've been to often digressed to men-bashing. I choose not to be part of that type of culture. I've also visited organizations where membership was primarily male, and found an "old boys' club" that was very hard to connect into as a woman. I much prefer

What type of networking events do you prefer to attend?				
	Structured networking meetings	Unstructured networking events	No preference, I like them all	Response Totals
Female	48.6% (2,886)	44.5% (365)	**53.1%** **(2,162)**	49.9% 95,413)
Male	**51.4%** **(3,058)**	**55.5%** **(455)**	47.0% (1,913)	**50.1%** **(5,426)**
Answered question	5,944	820	4,074	**10,838**
Skipped question				2

FIGURE 5.1—**Gender Preference for Type of Networking Event**

networking groups with a balance of men and women that respect and see one another as business equals—that's what I tend to find in BNI.

It's interesting that men expressed opinions about preferring both structured and nonstructured events. How linear can you get? If men like both types of events but express that by saying they prefer both equally, how is that different from the women preferring neither and liking them all? If you prefer neither and like them all, doesn't that mean the same thing as liking both? Both women and men are fine with both types of events, but the way they each expressed that is noteworthy. Does the greater flexibility of women reflect the current hypothesis that women naturally think with both sides of the brain, using the right ("creative") and left ("logical") sides together, where men favor one side? This respondent seems to think the female combination is a good formula:

I do think the attributes of women's brains allow us to instantly understand relationships and the underlying needs of prospective referrals that men may not see. It is my forte—connecting people with people. I attribute my many monthly referral awards at my BNI chapter partly to my female brain and its ability to farm for referrals for others.

♂ He Says . . .

These statistics do a good job showing part of the difference between men and women in business and life in general. Men said they preferred either structured or unstructured networking events. Women don't really care. They like them all.

As focused, results-oriented business professionals, we men like both structured networking meetings (like at BNI) or unstructured ones (like chamber mixers), but we need the meeting style to be defined before we get there so we can be prepared. We want to be able to put together a strategy or plan of attack, and plan for the types of rewards that are going to be at the meeting. If we know ahead of time, we can get our arsenal of tools ready to score goals, capture prey, or in general, just bring home the bounty. I'm pretty impressed with my gender's flexibility and ability to go with the flow and be open to both structured and unstructured events. I think it says a lot about our competency in rising to whatever occasion presents itself.

This finding is consistent with the male focus on our roles as providers. Both types of networking events have value to us; they just need to be attacked in different ways. Men have a variety of strategies to use for differing scenarios, and the two distinctive strategies we use on these events in particular are focused on producing the same results.

The structured event style is very appealing because it's predictable. Because I know what's coming, it allows me to put a system in place that keeps me focused on the end result. Structure means purpose. Knowing that the event program is stable allows me to measure, analyze, adapt, and change my strategic implementation on the move. Because we men tend to be more transaction-oriented and measure our success by the amount of business that we close, we like structure because it supports our constant intention to plan for and do just that.

Unstructured events are also very valuable because they leave a lot of the agenda up to me. For example, at a chamber of commerce networking event I sometimes decide to spend my time with the people I know well to build deeper relationships with them, but at other times I see a need to reach out and meet new people and develop new relationships. Or, I may decide to do neither and just hang out and see what happens. It is an opportunity to be seen, heard, and met in whatever way my creativity dictates for my current needs.

What this means is that as long as men are ready with a strategy that helps them achieve their overall goal, they'll be comfortable with whichever type of networking event they're at. Men want events that have a purpose and don't waste their time. Give men a well-run meeting and they'll be there whenever they can because they'll be confident about getting results.

She Says . . .

Author of *No Matter What*, Lisa Nichols makes a good observation: "I believe that men are interested in the results and women are interested in both the journey and the results."

If you've ever been on a car trip (or even an errand) with a man, you've experienced the meaning of the word "driven." Before you even get in the car he's mapped out the most efficient route to the destination, counted the number of times he'll need to stop for gas, and calculated the arrival time down to the minute. Then he loads his wife (or girlfriend) into the car and off they go. This typical scenario really shows how women love the journey and men love the accomplishment of reaching the destination:

"Honey, do we have to take the interstate? If we do, we'll miss so much of the beautiful countryside. Let's take some of those backcountry roads. Oh, look! There's a nice little shop. Let's stop and pick up a few souvenirs. Oh, and look at that lovely park. Let's stop and have a picnic."

You'll also see this love of the journey is reflected in the way women network and run their businesses. We want to slow down, build the relationship, and enjoy the process along the way. Both men and women are on the same road with ultimately the same destination, but the female tendency to stop and smell the roses may be partially responsible for why we live longer.

Type of Network

Women have learned from an early age to be flexible, which directly corresponds with their agreeableness to both structured and unstructured events, preferring neither over the other. Because of our many responsibilities, and out of necessity, we've developed the ability to change gears quickly. We may have planned a perfectly lovely day, but suddenly find ourselves in the middle of chaos, trying to juggle all the balls. Women are adaptable, fluid, and flexible collaborators and multitaskers. Does it really matter to us what kind of networking event it is? As long as we can figure out how to make it fit into our already hectic lives, we are happy to take part in it because we know we have the power to create something good from it.

We shouldn't be surprised that men are decisively choosing one event over the other, even when both are fine with them and they're really just choosing both. They'd much rather choose both than say that either one is fine. Do men see flexibility as weakness? Having an opinion surely is the opposite of wishy-washy. Ask him his opinion about anything and it is almost always an either or answer.

Because women are more fluid and flexible, when it comes to choosing our networking activities, we are perfectly at home in both. I stress the importance to my clients of being active in multiple types of networks as a way to diversify. If I am only a member of a structured network and never participate in any other type of networking, then I bring less to the table as a networking partner. I also caution all my clients to be careful how many organizations they join, because there will eventually come a point of diminished return once their time and attention is spread too thinly.

When I first started learning to network, I joined every single organization that I could. I was a member of a BNI chapter, six different chambers of commerce, my local Rotary club, a private club, and also went to every trade show in town hoping to make even more connections. It didn't take long for me to earn the nickname "The Queen of Networking," but what I actually learned from all that was that I was no longer getting results from any of my activities. I was networking wide instead of deep.

Whether you're a fan of structured or unstructured events really doesn't matter. What does matter is how thoroughly you develop your relationships in each of the organizations you connect with. Are you doing more than just showing up? Have you taken a leadership role in any of them? What is your investment beyond money? Good networking takes time. Ask yourself how much time you have to invest and where you'd like to invest it.

Women rated women-focused networking groups, such as NAWBO, E-Women, ABWA, and others, as their favorite places to network. There are several reasons why women prefer to belong to all-female networking groups.

- They want to network for more than business; rather, they want support and shared experiences with other businesswomen.
- Those who work at home want to be able to socialize and connect with other women.
- Many women are intimidated by men.
- Women are looking for female mentors and advisors with whom they feel more comfortable than male mentors.
- Many women feel, rightfully so, that men do not believe they are serious about their businesses.
- Women want to build relationships with other women.
- Women want to be able to address the whole slew of material they would not be comfortable addressing if men were around.

These are just a few of the reasons women seek all-female networking groups, as described by our study participants:

Earlier in my career, I belonged to an executive women's service club. During that membership, I was fired from a very good job. I went to the club meeting with my tail between my legs, stood up to introduce myself as we always did for each other, and told them about my day. By the end of the meeting, those women had three appointments for me for new jobs! It was wonderful.

Women enjoy and gain confidence networking with other women; some women (especially younger women) are still intimidated by men in mixed business networking groups. Some men still question why we started a group for women and why can't they have one for men. They forget that "old boys'" groups have been in operation for a long time.

I am on the board of directors for the Professional Women's Council, a division of the chamber where every other week approximately 90 women meet and network. There is definitely something to be said about the energy in that room! The women who are dedicated to the Council and attend regularly show such love and compassion for all the members. It makes doing business much easier!

My women entrepreneur network feels like a true support network.

While there are many women who love networking with all-female groups, there are just as many who do not. Here are some of their comments:

I found women-only events to be very poor and not what I would truly consider "networking." If you cannot communicate with the opposite sex, maybe you should reconsider your suitability for business.

As a woman, I prefer attending a networking meeting that has at least 50 percent women in attendance.

There are those of us who love snow and mountains and those who prefer sunny beaches. There are also those who like both. It's just a personal preference. It is neither right nor wrong as long as people understand the expectations of the groups they join. If the purpose of the group is support, then make sure you understand that when you join.

The best referrals come from people you build relationships with. For women, the relationship part comes naturally. Just remember that you have to actually have the referral conversation with your network if you expect to get referrals.

Wow, there seems to be some confusion here! Men seem to forget that they have had all-male networking groups for a very long time. Rotary International has been all-male since it was founded in 1905 and did not vote to allow women into its very prestigious network until the late 1980s. Unlike the women-only groups of today where men are welcome to join, few actually do but all are welcome. Take a look at the comments participants made about women's networking groups:

Some women's groups are against men in general and I don't agree with that at all. I think it is always nice to interact with people of both sexes.

I find it extremely insulting when a woman tells me she belongs to a "women only" networking group. It excludes 50 percent of the working population.

Since I began networking, I have come across many women's groups. I find it somewhat offensive to exclude men from these groups. If men did such a thing, women would make a scene about it. I think women and men should work together for mutual success. We no longer live in the 1950s. We need to live in the here and now.

I feel that there are too many women-only networking groups. I'm sure the women would object if there were men-only groups. I much prefer mixed groups.

Men, you are always welcome to join, if that's what you really want to do. You can reap great benefits from that membership.

What happened to a jeweler named Edward is a good example of how this works. He was great at taking notes about the personal preferences of and dates special to the women who visited his store. He decided to join a women's group, hosted the women in his store, served as an officer in the organization, and donated his time and money. Think about it, who buys jewelry? Did you say women? Wrong. Most often men buy gifts for their women, such as wedding rings, anniversary gifts, and so on. Edward would send notes, make phone calls, and drop emails to the men in the lives of the women in his network (about what their ladies' preferences were). He not only was successful networking with the ladies, he also enjoyed it.

Here is another example of how this helped a male networker:

I am one of only four men in a women-focused business group of about 100 women. I have found that because there are only a few men in our group, when I speak, the others pay extra attention to what I say. But this only works if I keep my comments and thoughts to a minimum. If I start to dominate the conversation, the tone or attitude can change fairly quickly.

Being associated with a women's business group can be very effective but only if you are willing to take a nondominant approach and are comfortable letting women completely control the environment, as expressed here:

> *I love being the only guy at women's networking events, such as those held by E-women. They tend to be very receptive and curious about why I am there and give me credit for courage. Women tend to be better clients then men.*

Men who are networking with women need to remember that for them it is all about the relationship. When you walk into an all-female group, you have to remember that you are in their world. Don't think for a moment that we cannot see through the man who is just trying to sell us. Look at what big mistakes these schmoozers made:

> *I used to belong to a women's business group. A male insurance agent attended. He assured us all, multiple times, that his best customers were women because he understood them so well. We were rolling eyes at the first repetition, and by the sixth or seventh, we were no longer listening. Setting yourself up as an expert on someone else's minority is not good networking.*

> *I used to belong to a women's business organization. There were more than 50 women who came on a monthly basis to develop relationships. At one point, a man decided he wanted to join the organization to sell health insurance to all the women. Very few women purchased his service, and he soon left the group. They felt he was only there to sell his services, then move on to the next group. He didn't take the time to actually become part of the group by volunteering on the board, giving back to the members, or building the relationships that could soon turn into long-term referral sources. He truly could have built his business through this group of women. Instead he was very narrow-minded and only thought about how he could benefit from being a member of a women's business group.*

Guys, be honest with yourself about the groups you're thinking about joining. Don't go into them unprepared to make commitments.

Whether your groups are all male or female, or mixed, none will work if you don't learn the appropriate skills. We can be successful networking, regardless of the organization we choose to join, if we do it the right way, without shortcuts.

The Survey Says . . .
Important Characteristics for Referring

For women, the most important factor when referring business to others was a person's competency, and for men, character (see Figure 5.2). Even though a person's competency was more important to women than to men, how successful that person was carried more weight with men. It is not clear how men and women distinguished between these two closely-related factors, except perhaps that men felt a person's competency was measured by the degree of success attained, and that essentially men and women were talking about the same thing.

Although by a lesser factor (under 20 percent), women were much more inclined than men to use the person's product or service before making the referral.

You can't judge a book by its cover, but you can judge strength of character and business development potential from a handshake.

When I first started out in business, I remember being advised to ensure that my contacts knew I was in business for real by ensuring that the first encounter should begin with a firm handshake. I've been told a number of times by businessmen that I have a good, strong handshake, and that it tells them I mean business—not like most women they meet.

Maybe, when you reflect upon that statement, it could have more than one meaning.

A strong handshake indicates a no-nonsense individual, straight to the point, let's get on with the business—and I have to say for the most part that's very true.

Less successful introductions for me have been with individuals who had weak handshakes.

There is no doubt about it from my experience that those with whom I have forged strong business links have been owners of the firm handshake. Maybe the subconscious takes over. It's strange, but true.

Assessing a person's character, competence, and success, among other attributes, is usually a pretty subjective task, of course. For some

Which of the following is most important to you when referring business to others?			
	What is your gender?		
	Female	Male	Response Totals
Knowing a person's character	38.8% (2,154)	42.8% (2,371)	40.8% (4,525)
Knowing a person's level of competency	39.6% (2,201)	40.8% (2,264)	40.2% (4,465)
Knowing a person's success	2.2% (124)	3.5% (192)	2.8% (316)
Using their product or service myself first	19.4% (1,077)	13.0% (718)	16.2% (1,795)
Answered question	5,555	5,544	11,099
Skipped question			1,323

FIGURE 5.2—**Important Characteristics for Referring**

people, like the survey respondent above, something as simple as a handshake reveals all they care to know.

In a networking context, these assessments are a way to ensure credibility—as well as to protect the reputation of person X when he or she is referring person Y to person Z. It's fair to say that men and women both want to be able to trust that every referral they offer produces a positive outcome for everyone involved.

Ironically, competence is defined differently according to perception. Some individuals judge competency levels strictly by business or job performance. Others also feel that networking ability is an accurate gauge for overall professional or even personal competence. What one person views as competence, another may see as character. This quote below is an interesting take on that:

Some men mistake flirting for networking. Women don't need to be made to feel good by a person of the opposite sex in order to want to do business with them. Most women base their judgment on the strength of the person's character and their competency level.

♂ He Says . . .

This is interesting. We asked what characteristics were most important to people for deciding whether or not to refer someone. The four categories they responded to were: character, competency, perceived level of success, and trying their product pre-referral. Men scored highest in all of the four categories except for trying the product or service first. Hmmm.

Why would this be? I think the good ol' boys' club or all-male business world mentality is responsible for this. There is an unwritten law that we men trust each other until we find a reason not to. I assume that you are professional and honest. While I am getting to know you, I learn about your character, competency, and level of success. If during our courting period I feel comfortable with those three characteristics, then I don't need to try your product or service. However, if I feel you are not who you portray yourself to be (bad character), or you don't seem to be as knowledgeable about your product or service as I think you should be (competency), or you don't have the level of success I'm looking for, I'll never try your product or service anyway because the sale has already been lost.

This goes back to the idea that every networking scenario is an audition. Men, don't forget that judgment in business is cumulative. One bad action may ruin the relationship for a long time, or even forever. We need to remember that we are proving ourselves every time we communicate with others.

 ## She Says . . .

Knowing a person's competency level was the most important characteristic for earning referrals from women. Additionally, more women than men felt that they needed to try a product or service prior to giving referrals.

Neither of my male co-authors understood why women felt the need more than men to try products before standing behind referrals. I explained that over time women have been taken advantage of by salespeople, mechanics, tradespeople, and so forth, mostly because they did not know which qualifications to choose service people with.

Here is what author John Gray, Ph.D., had to say in an interview with Dr. Misner:

> She is not going to support something simply because somebody says she should. She is going to because of her own personal experience with it. She wants to personally endorse it. She wants it to come from within. By nature, women want a lot of evidence before they can embrace something.

It's much easier for women to choose an auto repair professional based on personal references, which is almost as good as trying the product themselves. Most women do not know the technical ins and outs of a car engine the way that more men do, therefore it's easier for a woman to get snowed at an auto repair shop, not knowing the lingo to detect lies with, etc.

Women are very good at sharing both positive and negative information about their experiences about products and services, and are happy to do so to help one another. Most companies know that if you want to generate good word-of-mouth with women, get them to try your products and services, and if they like them, they'll happily tell everyone they know about you. They'll also spread the word just as quickly if they're unhappy.

In his book, *She Means Business*, Grant Schneider has this to say about the power of female word-of-mouth:

Salespeople, managers, advertisers, and even potential dates, beware! All the knowledge and experience in the world won't compensate for a perceived lack of concern for your female customers' overall satisfaction. You might be able to fool a woman once, but you will never have the chance to do it twice. However, earn her trust and you will have a customer, client, employee, or partner for life.

Before the age of social networking, online referral, and customer review sites, when a woman needed to find a doctor or dentist, she would simply find out who her friends and associates were using and what they had to say about that person.

Little has changed today. Women still storytell their experiences with products and services to other women. Women value the referrals of others so much that they even pass them secondhand, carrying along a hefty experience that happened to a friend, like this one:

I had to hire someone to come into my home and give it a good cleaning after I had a lot of remodeling and repair work done. I started asking my friends if they knew of a service that would clean the house well with earth-friendly products. Several of my friends told me secondhand stories from their friends and families, rather than relaying experiences they had actually had.

The message here is that it is more important to have a really good referral at hand that people are standing behind 100 percent than to have a referral of your own to give. If I do not have a personal reference to give, I at least still want to direct a friend to outstanding service, so whatever recommendation is the strongest creates the legend, and we pass it on.

A sticky wicket presents itself with networks of friends and associates. They trust each other and count on that trust and often ask for recommendations, but if I am not certain of their competence, then I am likely not going to refer them, friend or not, and if I do decide to refer them I'll add the caveat that I have not personally used them and it is not as strong a referral.

Men ranked knowing a person's character as the most valued quality when deciding on whether or not to make a referral. I don't concur, because I know people with great character, and like them a lot, but would never recommend them because they aren't competent at what they do. Those are two very different things, exclusive of one another, and one is not a reliable indicator of the other. The last thing a woman wants to do is recommend someone who doesn't work out well. That is a reflection on her. Because we women do so much mixing of business and pleasure of course we take all our relationships very personally. Men will just say, "Oh, it was just business" because they compartmentalize their relationships, but women will take the failure of the referral as a personal failure.

For most women it is never "just business," and the man who thinks that he can treat a woman that way or write the failure off as just business puts the entire relationship at risk. As stated earlier in the book, women speak to relate, to build the relationship before the business. But time after time men will say, "Hey, it was just business."

When I refer someone and that referral goes bad, I feel personally responsible for it. There will not be a second chance, and I will go out of my way to make it good with the person who was referred. It is personal and not "just business."

The Survey Says...
Comfort Levels with Networking

Over the many years of running a networking organization, I have heard comments from people saying that men are more naturally networkers because of their personal experiences or that women are more naturals at it because they are better communicators. These sentiments were only a few in the midst of all kinds of other opinions about why either men or women are more comfortable with networking. The truth, based on the survey results, appears to be that both men and women are close to equally comfortable. When we combined "somewhat comfortable," "very comfortable," and "loves to network," women and men scored almost identically to one another, with a total of 94.1 percent and 94.4 percent, respectively.

These respondents probably said it best when they stated:

Most of my business life has hinged on my ability to network comfortably with both men and women. Being able to put someone at ease, establishing open lines of communication, and following up in a timely fashion has created the best referral partnerships. Being able to give as well as receive in these relationships is the best of all possible worlds. Women sometimes think it is harder to deal with men, but it is important to remember that both parts of the network just want to do a good job and be recognized for it.

I find that men are very comfortable networking with me. The men and women I have met are equally happy networking with businesspeople of either gender.

I actually feel more comfortable networking with the opposite sex. I feel women working with women are more competitive.

Perhaps because I am extremely confident, I find that men are very comfortable networking with me, and certainly the men and women I have met through BNI in particular are equally happy networking with businesspeople of either gender.

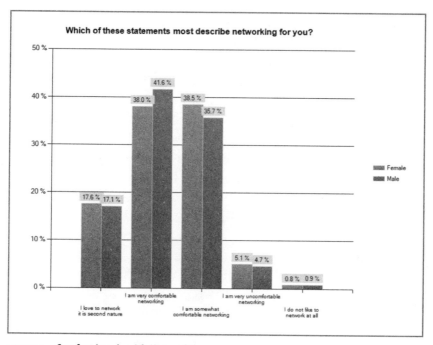

FIGURE 5.3—**Comfort Levels with Networking**

I generally feel more comfortable networking with women than men. I find I can relate faster and better with women than I can with men.

A very small percentage of people stated that they were uncomfortable or didn't like to network at all. However, despite the small number, they were a fairly vocal group. Both men and women talked about their discomfort networking as shown in the quotes below:

My physical impression on people is often intimidating, especially to women. I am young, not overly attractive, and built like a football player. Often, if I am approaching a woman who appears shy or seems intimidated, I try to buddy with someone else (preferably a woman) who is familiar with me. I let her make the introduction. Once the conversation starts it usually doesn't take long for someone to become comfortable with me.

When I first began my business, I joined the local chamber of commerce. Young, female, single, and naive, I frequently found myself in uncomfortable situations with men. What was presented as an invitation to dinner to learn more about one another's businesses frequently was little more than a social meeting with the hopeful undertones of a "date." It was insulting and frustrating. I actually began to shy away from business meetings with men since I could never be sure of their intentions when asking for a meeting. Soon after, I joined BNI and formed strong professional relationships with the men and women there. It gave me the knowledge and confidence to better control the environment of my business meetings so that there was never any question about the purpose of the meeting.

Which of these statements most describe networking for you?			
	What is your gender?		
	Female	Male	Response Totals
I love to network; it is second nature	17.6% (983)	17.1% (952)	17.3% (1,935)
I am very comfortable networking	38.0% (2,122)	41.6% (2,318)	39.8% (4,440)
I am somewhat comfortable networking	38.5% (2,149)	35.7% (1,990)	37.1% (4,139)
I am very uncomfortable networking	5.1% (285)	4.7% (262)	4.9% (547)
I do not like to network at all	0.8% (46)	0.9% (48)	0.8% (94)
Answered question	5,584	5,569	11,153
Skipped question			1,269

FIGURE 5.4—**Attitude Toward Networking**

5 / Alternate Perceptions, Differing Preferences

I find one-to-ones more uncomfortable with the opposite sex. Being seen in public by people who may not know it's strictly business is a concern that I try to deal with by adding others to the meeting. Having three or four people diffuses the issue. My time for obtaining information in this setting is compromised, but it's better than a damaged reputation.

I've recently started exploring my subconscious actions with regard to networking. My husband is uncomfortable about my networking with men, so as I get more male clients and referrals, I find I have unconsciously gained weight to make myself unattractive to them. On the one hand, this makes my husband more comfortable, but on the other hand, I miss my sexy curves.

Uncomfortable Networking with the Opposite Sex

We wanted to know how comfortable the survey respondents were when networking with people of the opposite sex. We thought there was a possibility that there might be a difference between men and women on this issue. Interestingly, there was not a significant difference at all.

In evaluating the data and having discussions with my co-authors, we started wondering if a person's impressions of others is different from the impressions they leave on others when it came to networking

Statement to rate: I am uncomfortable networking (by gender).

	Female	Male
Never or Almost Never	87.4%	88.8%
	(4,843)	(4,898)
Sometimes	7.4%	5.2%
	(410)	(288)
Always or most of the time	5.2%	5.9%
	(287)	(327)
Totals	5,540	5,513

FIGURE 5.5—**Networking Comfort**

with the opposite sex. Consequently, we conducted a much smaller, secondary survey asking people how they thought others felt about networking with the opposite sex and oh, my, were the results different.

Although the secondary survey had far fewer people, the results were dramatically different. Off-the-scales different. Comparing these two data sets (Figure 5.5 compared to Figure 5.6), we found that people were four times more likely to think that "other people" were always or mostly uncomfortable networking with people of the opposite sex compared to their own comfortable levels. Each person felt comfortable with it, but didn't think other people were.

This clearly indicates that our personal beliefs about our networking persona, or how we come across, versus our actual projected image or practices don't match. We see ourselves differently than the way people see us!

We may strive to build and create a public image that seems like a reflection of our personality and ethics, and think that naturally others see us through the same lens. We may think we're seen at networking events based on an idea of our communication skills, how we visually

Statement to rate: Do you think the average person is uncomfortable networking with the opposite sex?	Female	Male
Never or almost never	47.8% (4,843)	47.7% (4,898)
Sometimes	31.5% (410)	32.2% (288)
Always or most of the time	20.7% (287)	20.2% (327)
Totals	257	258

FIGURE 5.6—**Perception of Others' Networking Comfort by Gender**

come across and in general are received by people. But the way people see us is often very different than our intended image and message.

In conclusion, most of the people in our survey believed themselves to be more comfortable networking than everyone else, which follows the idea that the opposite sex in the networking arena has a different perspective on us than we do on ourselves.

♂ He Says . . .

According to the data, we believe that more than 32 percent of the people out there are uncomfortable networking with their gender counterpart. Why does each person in the survey rate themselves as more comfortable than everyone else? Neither the numbers and ideas about ourselves nor the perception of the discomfort of others add up.

My theory on this disconnect is that men are not as good at networking with the opposite sex as they believe they are. Many of us think we are doing well, but we are actually stepping on a lot of female toes. When we see other men doing it, we're thinking, "I am glad I don't do that and am better networking than they are."

Men have become too comfortable. We've been doing it for so long that we don't think our seasoned experience needs any improvement. We're very wrong about that and are part of that 30 percent who are not comfortable. This perception is in the eye of the beholder. If we continue our transactional approach to networking, just focusing on closing deals, we fail to build relationships. Over the long term this means we will always have to kill what we eat. That, guys, is a lot of work. Let's get smart like the women and grow our next meal!

Men may believe they're doing a great job networking because they're closing deals, but are possibly leaving a trail of annoyed people in their wake, because they don't seem to care about them. Women are wired to care about others and build real relationships, but we are not. We have to work at it. When we go out, it's with the purpose of bringing something home. This is a great way to stay focused, but our shortsightedness may hurt us in the long run. It is clear that others do not see us as comfortable. Remember that their perception is their reality, right or wrong.

Our confidence and comfort needs to be viewed critically and cautiously. Just because you're comfortable doesn't mean others are comfortable with you. Does it matter what other people think? In the networking game, which is all about building and developing our reputations, it matters very much. Let me repeat it here, if you missed it before, my perception of you is my reality of you!

The only way we get better is by continually self-assessing, analyzing, and critiquing. Look for feedback, visual cues, and how receptive people are to being around you. Networking meetings are a perfect place to do this. We need to make sure that our comfort level matches the level of comfort others feel around us. Maybe your levels already match up. Then again—maybe they don't.

 ## She Says . . .

When surveyed, 94 percent of both men and women said that they were comfortable networking, but my experience working with men and women tells a different story. Going to events and meeting people allows me to help others in my network. I ask people questions and listen as they tell me about their struggles and needs so that I can point them in the right direction, to the right people in my network.

It is when I set aside my own needs and step into the room with the intention of helping others that suddenly the networking becomes far more comfortable. I feel very successful when I am able to give referrals to members of my network. Networking goes far beyond the networking event. You have to also get comfortable with one-to-one conversations with people in your network post-meeting.

Most women nurture by nature. When that nurturing approach is applied to our networking activities it allows for a level of comfort that isn't there when we are being too pushy, asking others to just buy, buy, buy, from us. When I plan to attend an event, I have prewritten on a

3-by-5-inch card what I am trying to accomplish there. It may also list ideas for a possible connection for someone in my network, a referral for a referral partner, or a goal to meet one person who I would enjoy getting to know better and want to add to my network.

When I accomplish these goals at each event, I not only feel comfortable, I also feel successful. The more we use systems like this, the more practice we get at meetings and comfortable we become. Success follows thereafter as a natural reward. You will not get comfortable if you are not practicing. Get out of your office and go meet someone new today.

Gender Networking Discomforts

The word "networking" conjures a very commercial feeling and is often confused with selling. When I ask women if they're comfortable networking, they usually reply with something like this: "I can do it, but it's just not my favorite thing to do. It's so sales-y!" I believe the biggest issue really involves the word "networking." Most people think of it as the act of going somewhere to mingle in a room full of other people, shaking hands, giving elevator pitches, and handing out business cards.

While this is part of networking, there are so many other elements to it. Meeting with another person at a coffee shop to learn more about each other is networking. Meeting with an organized small group of businesspeople in order to help one another is networking. Serving on a board and volunteering with a group are both networking, as are chatting with people in the grocery store line or at the PTA meeting.

For those people who stated that they were uncomfortable with or disliked networking, taking another look at the definition of what networking actually is could be a great help. By and large women network naturally, and it is not until the business spin is enforced on it that they become uncomfortable.

Becoming comfortable with networking requires that we learn more about it, practice it more often, and change our mindset about what it is. When we apply the "Givers Gain" approach to it, we become completely comfortable. We are always more comfortable when we are helping others than we are when we are helping ourselves. It is the nature of women to help.

How Do You See Others?

I was at a loss with the results from our data when I first read them. I can't believe so many people say they are never or almost never uncomfortable networking, yet when we asked if they thought the average person was uncomfortable networking with the opposite sex, suddenly the whole thing took a turn. We saw that they felt everyone else but they were uncomfortable.

We see ourselves very different than we see others. This is human nature. We always see ourselves as different, regardless of how much alike we really are. I perceive myself as someone who is completely comfortable networking with either sex. But I don't believe people around me are comfortable at all networking with the opposite sex. Why is that? Are we fooling ourselves? So it stands to reason that you see yourself as completely comfortable, but you don't see me as being that comfortable networking with the opposite sex.

Here's the kicker: Does it really matter how comfortable we think we are if we're not producing results? Comfort just means I can go out there and meet people, not that I know how to generate business from those relationships. As a woman, I am completely comfortable at creating relationships. I don't know if they are always the right relationships for my goals, or if I'm having the right conversations with the right people at the right time, but I am comfortable building relationships.

If I see myself as comfortable, but others do not see me as comfortable at all, then what is the message I'm putting out there? What effect is it having on my ability to build my network? If we are going to get results, we must be able to connect to one another. If others see me as uncomfortable, then I may be doing something wrong, or putting out the wrong signals. It is important that I'm aware of how others perceive me. We're all friends, ladies, so ask a couple of your friends if they think you're comfortable networking. If they say no, then it may be time for you to find a coach or program to help you out.

6

What Steers Male and Female Networking Inertia?

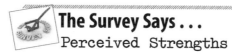

The Survey Says...
Perceived Strengths

Figure 6.1 on page 156 shows that more women than men believe their skills in connecting with others and developing quality relationships are strong. Women led the way in perceiving their strength at meeting new people, though only slightly more than men. The men's answers revealed their perceived strength in completing the cycle of networking by converting social connections into professional ones and ultimately, business opportunities.

These responses reflect the female tendency to focus on and develop the social much more than the transactional opportunities in networking. They also demonstrate the

What do you feel is your greatest strength in networking?					
	Connecting other people	Developing quality relationships	Good at following up	Meeting new people	Turning relationships into business opportunities	Response Totals
Female	**53.8%** (1,604)	**51.6%** (2,035)	46.5% (701)	**50.3%** (1,107)	39.8% (565)	49.9% (6,012)
Male	46.2% (1,376)	48.4% (1,908)	**53.5%** (805)	49.7% (1,094)	**60.2%** (855)	**50.1%** (6,038)
Answered question	2,980	3,943	1,506	2,201	1,420	12,050
Skipped question						0

FIGURE 6.1—**Perceived Greatest Strengths in Networking**

male tendency to jump more quickly into converting networking connections into transactions, and their focus on following up.

♂ He Says . . .

Interestingly, both men and women rated their greatest strength within networking as developing relationships. Does this mean that just because men and women put an equal value on developing relationships that we view networking relationships the same? Think again!

Though we do both find them important, we don't define networking relationships in the same way. Noting that men and women have different motivators for developing business relationships is important in understanding each group.

Men have been goal-oriented to the end means of problem solving as hunters and providers through time. The survival skill and added drive for quick and easy, efficient and effective, has remained over time. A perfect analogy to show how men move through a networking cycle is the cycle of purchasing goods or services. Initially there is a problem that needs to be solved, which is ultimately resolved by the emotional influence of what we hope to achieve with our purchase.

She Comments . . .

Anyone who has ever watched a guy troll the aisles of Home Depot has seen this theory in action. Make some popcorn and pull up a chair, ladies!

He Responds . . .

The same emotional motivator—carving out a status position—drives purchasing and networking. We men are always jockeying for the alpha position within our tribe. One of the most powerful ways to do this is by building and massaging relationships. The forming and maintaining of relationships is the most powerful tool I can use to create a position of status for myself in both my business and personal life.

Behind every successful business professional there is a history of teamwork and a social structure that supported, funded, or afforded his or her climb to the top. Because I am constantly aware of how these structures control my success, I will always make use of the "tools" at my disposal to update and elevate my male status position.

There are several ways I can form relationships that will contribute to my success.

Strategic Categories

- *Efficient, streamlined strategy.* I am always evaluating the most efficient way to operate within my primary, secondary, and tertiary relationships to elevate my status. I'd like to accomplish this as quickly and effortlessly as possible.

- *Relationship development.* If I take my current relationships to a higher level, they will be more productive to my success.
- *X-factor relationships.* These pleasant surprises are those relationships that by accident occur and become trusted, strong bonds that support my success.

Once these strategies are identified as tools to dominate the tribe with, we males get our action plan ready and head out for the hunt.

If I don't keep adjusting my hunting methods to the most efficient methods at my disposal, I'll be wandering around forever, just looking for my prey. I also set criteria to prioritize my prey so I don't waste energy on things that don't get me ahead.

PREY CRITERIA

- My prey must be a relationship in one of my strategic categories.
- They must be willing to assist with my goals.
- They have the relationship connections I need to elevate my status.
- They have the tools or access to what I need to solve my current problems.

After all this logical strategizing, I head deep into the jungle for the hunt. My instincts are honed to the single-minded goal of bringing home the kill. As I head to the known gathering area for my prey, I see multiple herds gathered together, camouflaging their choice members— those who will be valuable to me.

She Comments . . .

Hey, Tarzan! Don't forget to bring home a gallon of coconut milk while you're out there.

He Continues . . .

My hunting prowess kicks in as I sort through all of the wannabes, imposters, and unproductive types. I shall identify and isolate those powerful and pertinent to providing the best meat for my family, and then zero in, full force, on what I want. I will not be stopped or deterred by the challenge of finding the jewels hidden among the rest. I am a hunter, provider, and the strongest of my tribe.

Wow. We sure are a strange breed. Believe it or not, what I've just illustrated is largely the truth about male thinking, even if shown by humorous analogy. This really is the way we men think when we're networking.

What does this mean for you women?

It means that if you want to build a productive relationship with a man you must keep in mind where he is coming from and what his goals are as the provider, protector, and hunter of his domain. Begin conversations with men in the transaction mode, keeping the communication about business. This will start the bonding process and allow you to transition with him from hunting mode into relationship mode. Remember that he is hunting for valuable relationships. Once he sees your value, you're in like Flynn.

What does this mean for us men?

It means we're being idiots! People aren't just transactions or pirate booty just to be used for our gain. Remember that while you're so busy monopolizing the networking process with your thoughts about what you can get from that person, every deal you close in that mode will cost you five times its value.

When you network with women, you must first focus on the human relationship. Stay away from the transaction phase and just focus on growing the business friendship. If you don't, you'll lose sales, beneficial introductions, and referrals that can really affect your bottom line.

If you want to have productive male and female relationships, they must be mutually beneficial. Evolution has taught us that groups that communally hunt, catch, and share their wealth process benefit from their combined greater strength as a group over that of the individual. Some days your hunt will be fruitless and others will yield wealth. If we share, we all benefit.

She Comments . . .

Does this mean I can use the remote now?

She Says . . .

We've pointed out many times that women are relational and believe building relationships is primary and business connections secondary. We know that men see the business connection as primary, and after all, it is called business networking, so I can't blame them for that.

Because we women are already very good at connecting in a social way, you can see why we gravitate toward the relational activities of meeting new people, developing quality relationships, and connecting people to one another; something that is also called matchmaking. We are natural born matchmakers and have been doing this since time began. I think it may even be in our DNA. It's no great surprise that we excel in related activities.

He Comments . . .

I could live another day if I didn't get fixed up on one more blind date with one of your cousins.

She Continues . . .

Everyone I network with hears the same important question from me: "What can I do to help you in either your life or business?" The response from women is usually that they can't think of anything right now, but will let me know when they do. Men, on the other hand, will say, "Refer people to my business." I find both answers humorous.

Neither group really knows what to ask for because they don't know what goes on behind the scenes, though there are many things I can offer to help them with. A man asking that I refer potential clients to him even though I have never used his service is bold because I have no real relationship with him and this may be the very first time we've met. I applaud his courage but I only refer connections who've earned a spot over time through solid relationships and great service on my "trusted referral sources and partners" list. I need to believe in the person I refer and this understanding takes time to reveal itself.

It's a wonderful skill to be able to confidently reach out and connect to others in an effort to build strong relationships, but leveraging already proven relationships for business gain will always be favored over investing in new acquaintances.

Women's strengths lie in not only building relationships, but also in meeting new people and connecting everyone together for collaboration, using our wonderful matchmaking skills. Since the beginning of time, women have been at the core of forming the social structures of communities, beginning with our caveman and cavewoman roots. Modern-day business life finds us using those same natural assets to create true meaning in our professional relationships. If we can learn to add some of the strengths that men have to our toolbox, we will be invincible.

He Comments . . .

Hey, I like it when you talk like that!

The Survey Says . . .
Gender Weaknesses

When both sexes were asked to rate their weakest features in the networking process, their answers reflected the same results as when asked to rate themselves by strengths in the previous group of questions. Figure 6.2 on page 162 shows that men consider themselves weakest at continuing the conversation after a few minutes and approaching someone for the first time. Women felt their greatest weaknesses were being able to turn relationships into business opportunities, using a follow-up system, and knowing how to gracefully close a conversation. Our respondents wax on that theme here:

I'm very tired of networking for its own sake and finding nothing to hook onto. Everyone talks but nothing happens.

In general, I find men to be more "in your face" when it comes to networking. Women usually talk about everything but business when we first meet—we talk about movies, restaurants, family—and then we talk business. Men get to the purpose of the conversation faster, and while this probably makes the conversations shorter, it doesn't necessarily foster as much trust or strength for the relationship. The men I do tend to refer leads to are chattier, friendly types, because I feel I know them better.

I find it easier to speak to the opposite sex. Being able to build a personal relationship makes it easier to build a business relationship. When first speaking with men, a business relationship is easy to have. When first

What do you feel is your greatest weakness in networking?						
	Approaching someone for the first time	Continuing conversation after a few minutes	Knowing how to gracefully close conversation	Being unable to turn relationships into business opportunities	Using a follow-up system	Response Totals
Female	49.2% (1,344)	47.1% (429)	**50.4%** **(741)**	**50.5%** **(1,730)**	**50.4%** **(1,414)**	49.9% (5,658)
Male	**50.8%** **(1,385)**	**52.9%** **(482)**	49.6% (728)	49.5% (1,699)	49.6% (1,389)	**50.1%** **(5,683)**
Answered question	2,729	911	1,469	3,429	2,803	**11,341**
Skipped question						0

FIGURE 6.2—**Weaknesses in Networking**

conversing with women, they prefer that it not be all business. First they want to know what kind of person you are and if they have something in common with you. There is an unspoken approval process they go through before conducting business with you.

♂ He Says . . .

Men and women agree that their ability to turn relationships into business through networking is a big problem. Though we agree, we have different reasons for our similarities. Women are weak at closing the deal because they aren't particularly interested in doing so. Men rate themselves weak at closing the deal because of the high expectations they have set for themselves in that area. Do you see a pattern here?

The survey indicates men feel comfortable networking but don't see the importance of it in the grand scheme of their success; rather, they feel their inability to turn those relationships into business affects their success level more than networking.

We know men are transactional by nature and therefore see networking as a zero-gain game. Either we are making money right now, or we're not. If the return on the investment of time and effort is not clearly apparent, the activity is not worthwhile.

She Laughs . . .

Make THIS networking leap of faith, men! Picture a bunch of women fussing around a baby or looking at a photo album. Notice how fast any men in the vicinity vanish into thin air. Have you ever seen men move so quickly?

He Continues . . .

You never know. Most men are frustrated by their own low numbers of converting relationships into business transactions, not because it is an actual weakness, but because they set the bar to a goal inappropriate for what is going on. The best way men can achieve satisfaction in this area is to stop thinking of networking relationships as transaction goals.

We'll then not see our failure as a weakness, because it won't actually be a failure.

Men, set this key phrase to memory: You never know. You never know who's going to give you your next referral, when it will come, or who you'll meet and what role they'll end up playing in your life. You never know either how some favor or warm gesture you perform today will manifest a ripple into the future. It's impossible to predict.

If you believe all that fluffy "Give to the universe and it will give back to you," karma stuff is for the naive, let me share a true story with you to illustrate my very important point. The names have been changed for obvious reasons.

Let's Get Rid of Her, She's Not Worth That Much

Two months into helping start up a new chapter of BNI in Scarsdale, New York, the Membership Committee members met to talk about chapter growth and the kind of members we wanted in the group.

"Paul," a financial planner, said, "I think we should only focus on getting business owners in here whose companies have at least 10 employees."

I said, "That's not really what this is about. The whole concept here is to have a diversity of professions, company sizes, business ages, ages of professionals, etc. Basically it would be like the diversity we have now with our 36 members, but on a larger scale."

Paul strongly contended that what we currently had could be improved by getting "much better members in here."

"Better members?" I asked, with a cautionary raised eyebrow.

"Yes," he replied, "take Jacqueline, for example." The hairs on the back of my neck bristled.

"She doesn't own the business, and she's what, 21 years old? She's not going to be able to contribute very much to the chapter. We need someone who has owned a business for years, makes great money, and has a high net worth," Paul concluded, proudly making his case.

"Sounds to me that you're more focused on what would benefit you than the group. She's a great person, a very good member, and we're keeping her," I firmly announced.

SIX MONTHS LATER

As the president, during a network meeting I directed our group's attention to the referral phase of our gathering and said, "Please stand up, state your name, who your referral is for, and the quick story behind it."

Jacqueline stood up and began talking about her best friend's dad passing away in high school, leaving her friend, Susan, and her brother and mother alone. "Three months ago Susan's mom died of cancer," Jacqueline continued, "and now that Susan has inherited the estate, she's not sure what to do with all the assets and asked if I knew of anyone qualified to help. I was excited to be able to help refer her to Paul because he's a great guy, so smart and good at what he does. I told her about how he helped me start a savings plan." Jacqueline went on to tell Paul that not only was she referring Susan, but that her inheritance of more than $2.5 million needed managing, and she needed advice on taking care of her and her brother in the process.

15 MINUTES AFTER THE MEETING

I noticed Paul and Jacqueline speaking, and when they finished, I walked over and heard Paul wrapping up the conversation with, "Okay, great. No problem. I'll give her a call and get together with her right away. Don't worry. I'll take care of her, and thank you for the referral."

When Jacqueline walked away I could not resist the urge to gloat, "You were right, Paul, we should have gotten rid of her six months ago!"

He dropped his head sheepishly, shaking it, and said, "Oh, my gosh. I feel like such an idiot."

I couldn't help but drive the point further home, "You should, Paul. You never know. You just never know where that next referral is going to come from. Have you ever received a referral from anyone else in this group of that size?"

"Nothing even close," he replied.

I asked him if he'd ever received a two-and-a-half-million-dollar referral from anyone at all.

"No. Never," he stated.

"Never judge someone based on what you think you can get from them today. Relationships are long in the making and are about building long -term success. You never know who people are connected to or where your reputation will take you. You just never know," I said, and walked away.

♀ She Says . . .

Because we women consider building relationships one of our key strengths, the fact that we consider our weakest link the perceived inability to convert relationships into business should come as no surprise. Here is a comment that was left on my blog by a reader:

> I'm a new small-business owner with potential for huge growth. People who know me well describe me as outgoing, confident, strong, good with people and knowing what I want and how to get it. I'm passionate and intense about what I believe in and do, however, I am finding it very difficult to ask for referrals or help of any kind even from those I have known for years. I have worked with church groups in the past and have had to basically beg for others and did it. I just can't ask for what I need for myself. Why is this?

She asked that question because it's confusing why women don't feel comfortable asking for things for themselves. We have this fear that others will think poorly of us, or we will be a burden or considered weak. We get confused about why we are networking. It's not just to build relationships. To build up our businesses we have to ask for what we need. People will not just magically figure that out and give it to us.

I was invited to speak to an audience of men and women about how they could get more from their networking efforts. I talked mostly about generating more business from networking events. When I finished and began circulating about in the foyer, a lot of people approached me with comments and questions. Interestingly, the women felt I'd spent too much emphasis in my talk on networking for the end means of business, when they felt the most important part of networking was to meet people and build long-term relationships with them.

One woman was very upset, feeling that I commercialized relationships. I asked her how she got more business. She said that when people got to know her and what she did, they chose her service. She stated that she did not have to sell her friends to get business. Conversely, more of the men thanked me for the information and wanted to know even more about how to leverage their networking time to create business.

The thing that stops women from leveraging their networking efforts into business is the asking step. This survey respondent's comment reveals that.

As a sales trainer I've noticed for years that men "ask for the sale" much more readily than women, who need additional coaching in this area.

One reason we take a very passive role in generating referrals through our networks is that we are very protective of our clients, preferring to take care of them ourselves rather than connecting them to others who may not treat them as well.

This weakest link for women, not converting connections into business, extends beyond immediate referrals. We also avoid asking our networks for referrals or help growing our businesses. We have to believe in our own worth, and know that when we ask for connections, referrals, and business, we are worth it. All too often women tell me they don't feel like they deserve to ask or they don't know what to charge. Many women have a very low opinion of their own worth and that makes it very hard to ask for what we want.

He Comments . . .

How come we're always the ones getting flack for not asking for directions?

She Responds . . .

Good point!

When I teach 18 Ways to Motivate Your Referral Relationships to my clients at the Referral Institute, both men and women are enthusiastic about implementing the techniques immediately within their networks.

When I move on to the 15 Ways Others Can Help You phase of training, the men embrace the 15 activities, but the women give all kinds of excuses, such as, "I could never ask people to do things like this for me," or "It would be very uncomfortable for me to impose this on people." I have to remind them that they'd only be asking for help from their closest relationships and wouldn't be asking anyone to do anything they wouldn't be happy to do in return. I also remind them how happy they were to get to work on the 18 things I just asked them to do for other people!

Even though women understand the cycle of giving before getting, there is a queasy resistance to the asking phase because, as one respondent expressed, "I don't want people to think that I am giving to them just so they will do something for me." The asking part of the cycle is difficult to embrace. Oh, if we were only as good at asking others to help us as we are at helping them.

He Comments . . .

For some reason, I'm remembering my Aunt Harriet holding down a job and raising six kids by herself. This whole time I thought she was just this completely self-sufficient wonder woman, she also could have been desperately wanting help, but wasn't so great at asking for it.

She Continues . . .

A great example of someone who isn't afraid to reach out and ask for what he wants is Kevin Eikenberry, a longtime member of my network. It had been some time since we'd spoken so when he contacted me, we quickly got caught up on personal chat and then got down to business. He wanted me to read and review his new book, then post it on my blog if I liked it and thought it was valuable. He then asked if there was anything he could do for me. Instead of responding with the old, "Nothing right now, but I'll let you know," I asked him to do the exact same thing for me when my own book came out. He said he was more than happy to help promote it.

Kevin had no issue at all asking his network for help promoting his book. On the other hand, another member of my network has also written a book and never asked for any help.

Women are confused about the definition of business networking partially because the initial phase of general networking is neutral and can later yield both personal and professional results. We tend to blur the line between our business and professional relationships and place greater importance on personal over professional relationships, so it's natural that general networking deviates to a personal standing in our minds.

It's a given that we prefer to refer business to those we like and trust. But that doesn't mean that we're going to continue to blur the line once the business relationship is up and running, going to one another's family reunions and baby showers together. It does mean that we need to define that difference between personal and professional in our relationships by asking. Asking takes the relationship to a level it won't go to if that step isn't taken. Ladies, rev up your engines and start asking!

Another missed opportunity to ask is this classic example of over-thinking the personal part of a relationship: My coaching client, Brenda, was angry one afternoon when she arrived for her usual appointment. She flopped herself loudly into a chair and threw up her hands in exasperation, blurting, "I don't even know why I'm in the T-shirt business! I think I'm just going to close up shop and be done with it!"

As our conversation progressed, I discovered that a networking associate of hers had placed a rather large order of T-shirts with one of Brenda's competitors. She was hurt, disappointed, and angry. I asked her if she had ever asked Heather, the networking associate, for business. She was first dumbfounded, and then replied incredulously, "Why would I need to ask her? She knows I'm in the T-shirt business! If she wanted to use my service, she would have. She clearly doesn't!"

We then called Heather to find out why she'd chosen Brenda's competitor. The answer was not at all surprising to me. Heather simply said, "Brenda has never asked for my business. She knows I'm on the board of a nonprofit and that we do this annual event that I needed the shirts for. I just assumed she didn't want to do business with nonprofits because she never asked to supply us with shirts."

He Comments . . .

If that were my connection, that nonprofit would have been sold some matching hats, too. Can you say cha-ching?

She Continues . . .

Lesson learned? Always ask! Even close connections who know what your business is may have confusion about using it. If you expect people to read your mind, you'll greatly reduce your sales. Heather had made an assumption based on lack of information, which is very common. Because Brenda didn't provide the clarity of asking, she lost the sale.

The chaotic idea of doing business with family and friends doesn't need to be so complicated. I continually hear the phrase "I don't like doing business with family and friends." But I wonder if those people are waiting for their family and friends to approach them for business. If that's the case, their own family and friends may think the business is unwanted because they have not been asked for it, so they keep their mouths shut, and on goes the chaos with the former thinking their business is also not desired.

He Comments . . .

I'm getting dizzy. This is kind of like being in a fun house—except for the fun part.

She Continues . . .

Women frequently tell me they're not comfortable commercializing their relationships. If women develop more personal, friend-like relationships than men with most people they meet, then who does that leave for them to do actual business with? No one wants to feel used, but that's a very different scenario from clearly defining your business goals. We must be able to define ourselves as professionals by asking, while still maintaining relationships. These two concepts can exist in the same universe. Asking gives a clear definition to those around us and is actually a gift that clarifies for them what we want. If you don't bother to tell the people you network with what you need, you won't get it.

Imagine how strong we will be as business owners when we combine our generosity to do for others with the enormous level of help we will get once we begin asking. Asking opens a door to be greater than we ever could have imagined.

The Survey Says . . .
Most Important Networking Characteristics

Both men and women tracked very closely in what they thought the top seven traits of a good networker were, as shown in Figure 6.3 on page 172. Both felt that "helping others" was the most important trait or characteristic of a good networker. This is a change from the survey I conducted more than a decade ago in which this characteristic ranked eighth in the *Masters of Networking*. I believe this is because of a gradually changing belief system with businesspeople that the best way to get business is to help other people get business. This shift in consciousness relating to what makes a "good" networker is a positive shift that shows a better understanding of how to make the process truly work more effectively for business professionals.

Being trustworthy was the second highest trait identified by both men and women. Trust is the foundation of a referral relationship and is key to the networking process. It is not surprising to see this so high in the results. Trust is the currency of a successful networking relationship.

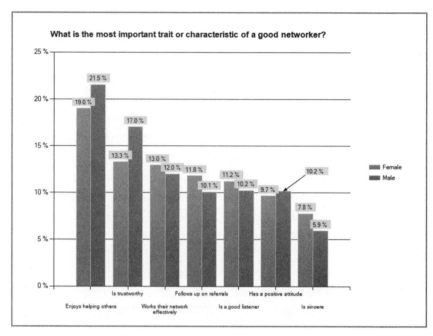

FIGURE 6.3—**What Is the Most Important Trait or Characteristic of a Good Networker?**

"Works their network effectively" was ranked next highest by both genders. On the other hand, women placed slightly more importance than men on following up, good listening skills, and sincerity. These priorities may be linked to the female prerequisite to develop a relationship before doing business. In other words, the preference for those traits supports the comfort level women create with "people," rather than "business leads."

Interestingly, more men than women voted that positive attitude was an important networking skill. While neither gender likes a chronic complainer, men may have less of a proclivity to dedicate time to emotional nuances. It's possible that men simply see negative networkers as energy-sapping, time-wasting, and unproductive, not to mention the red flag downer aspect.

One of our respondents argued:

Generalizing about men and women, rather than distinguishing between personality types, can be dangerous. I feel just as comfortable in a room full of men as women, unless they start talking about something I am completely disinterested in, like football. The same level of disengagement happens to me if I'm in a room full of women and they start talking about handbags, another subject I couldn't care less about. The most successful networkers just evaluate people as having a need, and then find the best way to help them.

♂ He Says . . .

This question is one that I feel we guys win! Here is the way we ranked the most important characteristics of a networker, and we are right!

1. Trustworthy
2. Likes helping others
3. Has a positive attitude

We men believe that if someone is a good networker they must first be trustworthy; second, be the type of person who likes to help others; and third, have a positive attitude. Is this a surprise to anybody?

If I don't trust you, then I may be friendly to you but don't consider you part of my true network. If someone makes it into my network it means I'm willing to work with them and refer and recommend them to others. Not everyone is going to be "the best" at what they do. Besides the fact that "best" is a subjective term, it is really meaningless. What I'm looking for is someone I can trust. I need to be able to trust them with my business, friends, family, clients, and associates.

I need to know that when I introduce this person to my inner circle of networking associates that he or she is going to deliver. If they don't treat my people right, they not only hurt their reputation with me and my network, but they've also hurt my reputation. This is not allowed!

I want to surround myself with people who are team players, people who understand that in order to achieve success in life you must first help others do the same. If someone doesn't like to help others then they just don't get it. They certainly don't get me. However, when I see someone who goes the extra mile, puts others' needs in front of their own—this is a person I want to be related to. This is a networker who is valuable not just to me but to everyone I have a relationship with. I believe in helping others and want to surround myself with people who feel the same.

Positive attitude? Duh! Of course. Who wants to hang out with negative people? We all have positive and negative stuff happening. Life offers all kinds of challenges on a daily basis. Sometimes the only way to get through them is with a positive attitude and support system around you of like-minded folks.

Business can take many hours and a lot of hard work. The more positive people you have around you, the better results you'll get because the more stimulated you'll stay, which will help you achieve more. Positive people inspire, motivate, encourage, and help in many ways.

See, ladies, we men are not so bad. Trustworthy, likes helping others, and has a positive attitude: You can't get much better than that, can you? I mean, we are looking for people who have these attributes, and that says something about us as a gender, yes?

Men, I would like to say how proud I am of you. There were many time I called us idiots in this book, but this time I can truly say we are very bright, talented, good-looking, funny, real, and down-to-earth. We done good here, guys—we done good!

♀ She Says . . .

The reason women rated good listening skills and sincerity higher than men did is because they are relational qualities. Most of the women I know share the desire for follow up after we've put hard work into creating a connection for someone. Once we refer someone, they are not only responsible for that task, they also have our stamp of approval, which is, in a way, a representation of us, as well as a voucher.

Because we are such multitaskers, spinning many plates at once, once we hand off one of those plates we certainly don't want to go back and find it was not taken care of. The last thing I want is to have to go back and follow up myself on a hard-won, carelessly dropped referral, not only because it's one more thing for me to do, but also because it makes my judgment appear questionable.

I've found that when I give a referral to men, they don't take it as seriously as I would like them to and have a tendency to take their time following up on it. This is also one of the most common complaints I hear from other women in my referral groups. We are also naturally curious and caring about how the referral panned out so we'd like to get a call about how it went.

Best-selling author Susan Roane gives men this valuable piece of advice for networking successfully with women:

Women love to share contacts, leads, information, and resources. An added benefit is that we will always want to know how it went, which is good follow up, because we are natural matchmakers and very responsive. But, though it may be kind of a racy analogy, if you just had a one-night stand with one of our friends, we'd want you to call and say it was wonderful. This advice is for both men and women. Just keep us in the loop! We women need that.

Another observation regarding the lack of establishing mutual understanding leaves women wanting to close yet another gap. Many women tell me they don't feel men are actively listening to them during networking. Because active listening is crucial to understanding, to building a solid relationship, and to ultimately making a sound referral, I recommend to men that they seriously start engaging active listening skills, especially with women. If you are not listening, you are leaving money on the table.

One of my biggest irritants in one-to-one meetings with men is their obsessive cell phone preoccupation. If they are so easily distracted by each text, missed call, and vibration this little machine makes, could they possibly really be present and listening to what I am saying? I rarely have this problem with women, and frequently do with men.

One night I was having a drink with a male business associate at a local bar. As we talked, not only did he check his phone, but also texted someone else through the duration of our meeting. Aggravated by his lack of courtesy, and feeling as if I was not being listened to, I asked if this was the way he managed all his relationships. He became defensive, but put the phone away for the rest of the meeting and we were able to finish up with pleasant conversation.

I sometimes think it's a news flash to men that we are uncomfortable with their lack of manners and how disrespectful it feels. It's also not conducive to getting to know and understand the person you've made time to meet. He obviously wasn't intentionally trying to annoy me, was he? He used the information I gave him and changed his behavior.

The responsibility for this one lies with both sexes. Gentlemen, put your phones away. Manage your other social responsibilities before you meet with us and honor our time together by respectfully directing your attention toward us. Ladies, ask for the behavior you want. Don't percolate in your own irritation. Let the guys know in a friendly way that you're there for the meeting and not to wait for him to take care of his extraneous admin on your watch.

He Comments . . .

Does this rule also include using my GPS while I'm on a conference call in my car?

She Continues . . .

I think most of us would agree that we are on our best behavior in the beginning of getting to know one another, wanting to put our best face forward. If this is the behavior I get in the beginning of a networking process, I've learned that it is a signal that the person isn't willing to listen, or even is incapable of it. Of course I don't want to connect that person with valuable resources!

Sincerity is the other attribute women ranked of greater importance than did men. There's nothing I dislike more than a fake. The insincerity is just dripping off of them as they try and charm their way into your pockets. We women run into this in business—that feeling that men are just in it for themselves, being cloyingly sweet to sell you something.

He Comments . . .

That kind of sounds like what happened with this very wealthy guy in his 90s I know who married a 22-year-old.

She Responds . . .

That's not what I'm talking about! But I agree, insincerity is disgusting wherever it's coming from.

Every woman has had the after-date experience where the guy says he'll call and doesn't. I remember a professional connection that left me feeling a little used, which I couldn't see from my vantage point until it was over. I had built a referral relationship with a guy who had a common target market, and we worked well with each other's clients. I arranged speaking engagements and gave him referrals. The relationship felt good. After about a year I was able to step back and see that his intentions were very insincere. He spoke of giving but his actions were only of taking. It didn't feel good, needless to say, but sometimes sincerity is a hard attribute to understand.

Though women ranked sincerity higher than men as a valuable networking trait, both men and women truly want it. We both hold out hope that the people we build connections with in the future will be sincere, don't we?

Networking Investments

The Survey Says . . .
Time Spent Networking

We asked a number of questions in the survey regarding time spent in networking activities. Both men and women devoted fairly similar amounts of time to these endeavors. When asked, "How many organizations do you belong to for the purpose of networking with others?" women averaged 2.47 groups and men averaged 2.58 groups. Hence, men belonged to slightly more networking groups on average than women did.

When asked how many hours per week they averaged developing their networks, men and women again responded with similar numbers. The overall average amount of time that people spent on networking activities was 6.31 hours. Men slightly outpaced women at 6.44 hours per week on average compared to women averaging 6.19.

Why do the numbers show women spending less time networking than men? Judging from respondents' comments, women appear to be very cognizant of and purposeful with the time they devote to networking, as we see reflected in the comments below:

Women tend to network less due to family obligations, especially those with young children.

Family time is precious, so I dedicate my networking time to business hours.

In addition, we've found that women generate more referrals from their networking efforts. In contrast, men appear to be less cognizant of and organized about their networking and expect results faster. We're finding that women are more organized and focused in their networking efforts, particularly if family needs are competing for their time, as expressed in the response below:

I've heard stories from other men who use networking as their primary method to get leads and sales. They quit organizations if they do not get significant business from them after a short period of time. Several have told me they quit after four to six weeks because they didn't make a sale. I don't hear the same things from women who network for business. If they quit, it's typically because they had other commitments, didn't like the personality of the group, or felt uncomfortable. I've never heard a woman tell me that because she didn't get business after four to six weeks she felt it was a failure.

Ironically, especially men who cling to a transactional approach think they're saving time by leaving a group they feel isn't paying off in an acceptable amount of time. They're hunting, jumping around, not letting their efforts gel. In other words, they're spending more time, but getting fewer results than women.

On the other hand, a woman in the survey had a very different take on the process, which demonstrates the time women are willing to invest in developing their connections for long-term results:

Both business and life in general are all about building and strengthening relationships. It is important to invest the necessary time to get to know the people and businesses and watch the way they conduct themselves and contribute to your life. Do they solve problems, add value, follow up in a timely manner, ask questions, listen with both head and heart, have the desire to learn about your business, make referrals, and THANK the referring parties? In addition, I feel strongly that it is important to be able to develop the art of giving and receiving business versus being one-sided.

Men are much more likely to see networking as, well, working. I have probably contributed to this attitude with influential language over the years by often telling newbies, "It's not net-sit or net-eat. It's net-work!" Men tend to see networking as a business-building task, while women tend to see relationship development as a necessary context within which business may someday be discussed.

Building relationships can be fun, exciting, and invigorating. So women who join multiple groups are probably having a good time, while recognizing that this activity they find so enjoyable is also very likely to lead to new business or professional opportunities over the long run.

Women find connecting with new people and experiencing different personalities interesting and pleasurable. You've probably heard the famous Forrest Gump line of the famed movie, "Momma always said that life is like a box of chocolates. You never know what you're going to get.'" In a networking context, you might say women like to try the bonbons. They enjoy the variety and sampling of different personalities. Perhaps they are easier to network with because they enjoy the social aspects of it so much more, as expressed in this networker's comment:

In general, women are easier to network with. They are more open to a discussion forum. At most of the social networking forums I go to, I tend to sit or talk with mostly women. Men tend to be easier to relate to in a strictly business manner first, then talk to about family or other social issues.

Men, on the other hand, tend to look for what they want in that box of chocolates and then go after it. Remember the guide in the chocolate box that tells which filling is in each chocolate? A man is more likely to look at the guide, and then zero in on the maple nut or cherry cordial, because that's exactly what they came for. Why waste time on the caramels and nougats when they're not giving him what he wants? They're not there to sample; they're there to hunt, and hunting for business is work—work best done in the one place most likely to yield good results.

♂ He Says . . .

As you know by now, we men are generally results-oriented and transaction-focused. Networking is a key factor to developing the strategic referral relationships that I need to bring home my bounty. My hunting grounds include a variety of casual contact, online and referral networks, service clubs, and women's business associations, because having access to many resources ups my chances for greater riches.

As men, we believe that if there is opportunity for business and we are serious about providing for our family or tribe, we must check out all of the hunting options available to us. Besides, variety is the spice of life, right? Even though we explore many options, we will not stay with any network for very long that doesn't show that it's contributing to our success. Why? Mostly because we don't have much of an attention span and need to keep our very simplistic minds occupied with the straightforward actions that will lead us to our goals.

Some of the networks I belong to I love, others, not so much. My fondness for the groups I belong to adds to the enjoyment of networking, and that's all very nice, but ultimately, I do what I have to do to keep generating business for myself. It is as simple as the men hunting to provide for their families only in areas where they know they'll bring home dinner. Why hunt where there's no action?

I want to be successful and I don't want to have to work hard. I'd rather work smart. I am not looking to build a relationship with the hunting grounds or geographical venues I use to hunt; rather, I just want to hunt and bring home bounty by using the area.

Male networking success is largely controlled by two tools: the variety of organizations we choose to belong to and the development of our own networking skills. That seems pretty simple, doesn't it? How difficult is it, really? I just go to a variety of events, talk to people, find out who they are and what they do, and then determine whether or not there is a match. If there's a match, I continue the relationship. If not, I don't. It's pretty black and white. This is what we men do. I'm sure you can see where I'm going with this: Yes. I'll reiterate once again that we men are idiots!

You men might be thinking, "Wait a minute, Frank, don't tell me this doesn't work. I have been in business and networking for years and have closed a lot of deals without wasting a lot of time."

I am sure you have, fellas. The question is, how many more could you have closed? If we are not continually educating and developing ourselves, we may become more experienced at networking, but it doesn't mean we are becoming more effective. In order to become better at something we must focus on three areas: our actions, beliefs, and knowledge.

Our Actions

These are the physical activities we do on a daily basis, e.g., making calls, emails, going to networking events, balancing our checkbooks.

Our Beliefs

This is the internal dialogue that we have with ourselves that tells us who we are. Do I feel confident? Am I being too pushy? What is the right thing to do or say? Is my product or service great or could it use improvement? Am I charging too much? I am sure you can remember many of the other questions that run through your head on a typical day and determine what you do next.

Our Knowledge

This is the intellectual understanding that we have of specific activities and topics. If you are trying to be an effective networker or salesperson, you should be asking yourself if you know about all of the current theories and methods of effective networking, such as The VCP Process®, The Strategic Revenue Cycle, Upfront Expectations Management, Strategic Alliance Teams, and Tier 1, 2, and 3 Referrals, to name only several. If these terms don't sound familiar to you, then it is likely that you need to increase your knowledge base.

An example of how those three facets come together to help achieve goals is demonstrated below in a "becoming a tennis player" scenario. It begins when I decide that I want to play tennis. I have never played before. I wonder: What is it that I have to do to become proficient at it? Then I set up the plan.

KNOWLEDGE

I need to study the game in all of its facets including the different types of strokes and shots, techniques for scoring points, and winning strategies.

ACTION

I need to take lessons and practice. The lessons will help me put to action the instructions I've read about playing tennis. I will then understand how to actually control where the ball winds up with knowledge of all of the strokes available and how to use them. My body will finally understand what my mind has processed intellectually. It will now allow my mind a deeper and true understanding, which also raises my intellect.

BELIEF

I need to build my belief in my tennis acumen and myself. The more confident I feel about myself the better I will be able to play the game. Without inner confidence it just won't happen. I may be good, but I will never be great without belief, and that belief is built in stages from seeing how I succeed over and over.

The same principles are true in developing your networking and business skills: You must gain the intellectual understanding of the particular topic matter at hand. You then need to go out and practice what you have learned. This will allow you to join book knowledge with real life. Most important, you need to develop the confidence for that skill so you become a true professional at it, and that comes with practice and effort.

You may wonder why I'm stressing these three building blocks so much when a lot of you reading this book have spent years in business and certainly know what you're doing. Well, you may know what you're doing, but you may just be doing the same old thing over and over. Of course you know what you're doing; you've had 20 years to practice it.

Too many men think, "Please. I have been doing this for years." There is a great old response to that which is, "So, have you been improving for 20 years or have you been repeating the first year over 20 times?" Men, let's get some humility and realize that we have to grow and get better at communication, relationships, and business techniques. Just because you've been using communication, relationships, and business techniques for years certainly doesn't mean that you're using them well.

You may just be working very hard using tools you're inadequately informed about. If I found you playing golf after years with a golf club and you claimed you were great because of your seasoned experience, imagine the surprise you'd feel if I pointed out that you were holding the club by the wrong end and how much better you could be if you were to turn it around. Good doesn't mean you can't get better. I guarantee that you can get better. By the way, when you use all the tools available to you at their full potential, you become a more skilled practitioner of your craft, and that means the returns on your investments are better with less time and effort spent. Now do I have your attention?

Why Do Men Spend More Time Networking?

Yes, I am a modern-day man, so of course I want "balance" in my life. But I want it all, including time to work and everything that encompasses, quality time with my kids, and alone time with my wife. But I see myself as the provider for my family. That means I will do whatever it takes to make my business successful. If I need to be somewhere to get business, I'll be there.

Do men spend more time networking than women? Yes. This is our cultural imperative. When my great, great, great caveman granddaddy a million years ago went to get food for his family, he didn't usually return home empty-handed. He just needed to do whatever it took to make it happen and however long that took; well, that's why they wore those furry one-piece get-ups—to ward off the chill on long hunts. Their very survival was dependent on him coming home with the food. Modern-day me feels the same way. I will commit and take the time that I need to be successful. If I go out and spend less time but don't come home with the prize, then what was the point? It takes as much time as it takes until I get what I came for. Then I can go home.

 ## She Says . . .

Our survey says that men spend more time networking than women do, but it appears that women get better results. At first this seemed a little confusing until I began to look at what women do compared to what the men do. Women call going to events to network, networking. When they are at a PTA meeting, a volunteer meeting, or sitting at a restaurant, they are socializing, and they do not consider this networking. When they play golf, they golf and socialize. While men on the other hand call most things networking, if you read what he said above, if they feel they can get business from it, it is networking. When they are on the golf course they are networking, when they are having dinner with a potential referral source they are networking.

Remember that women are more likely to be relational, they take their time, they look for common ground and find places that they can support and collaborate. Women have already said they do not like to commercialize their networks, so it stands to reason they also do not like to commercialize their social time. I have a magnet on my refrigerator, and I am certain many women have seen it. It depicts four women talking, and the caption says: "It is not gossiping, it is networking." Women socialize, they connect. Men always called it gossiping; often it was done over the back fence, it was relationship building. If you need something for your family, ask a mom. I wrote a short story in the book *Masters of Networking* called "Mothers are Natural Born Networkers." Nothing could be more true!

The next step in the progression for women is how to ask their networks to help them build their businesses. Women spend a great deal of time networking, but it is often unintentional. One of the ways to strengthen their networking muscle is to be intentional with their networking activities. Men often serve on boards as a way of connecting and networking, but women serve on boards because they care about the cause and often never connect their business networking to it. If we would be more cognizant of our network, we would realize that we have a vast array of people who can and will help us in our business.

8

Planned Systems Yield More Results

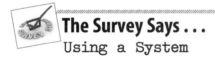

The Survey Says...
Using a System

Using a systematic approach to networking was the focus of several of the questions on the survey. Results were revealing in a number of ways. When we asked the people in the survey if they had a systematic approach for staying in contact with the people they met through networking, 58 percent of the respondents said "No." We had very similar results on at least one other related question. The difference between men and women in these responses was negligible and not statistically significant.

What is significant, however, is that most people don't have a solid system in place to guarantee that they stay in touch and ensure their connections are not dropped. This is a fatal flaw in relation to building a powerful personal network. We know this because our later survey results showed how influential the relationship between using systems and producing positive business results was, but we'll get to that soon. Notice in the quote below how the impersonal follow-up, or lack of a quality system, turns off the recipient:

I once attended a networking evening at which I was "sold" to by the men there. One of them was a car dealer. I was actually thinking of buying a new car at that time. I listened to his sales speech, told him I was very interested and gave him my card, asking that he call me. Two days later I got an impersonal mass-market email from him that he circulated to everyone he'd met. He never called me. What's the point of going to these things if you are not going to listen to the people you meet or follow up a hot lead?

Those who do use good follow-up techniques show how powerful solid follow-up systems can be. This couple, for example, discovered how to leverage one another's contacts:

My wife and I work together to bring referrals to each other. She is a banker and I am an online business consultant. Her keeping-in-contact system begins with asking her clients for their business cards. Then she asks them if they have a website, how they like it, and how they get business. She uses that opportunity to refer them to my web design, e-commerce, and online marketing services. In turn, I ask my clients if they use online credit card payment services for their businesses and use that as a segue to introduce them to the services my wife provides as a personal banker.

This respondent also recognizes the importance of having a systematic approach:

I have a very extensive (yet monitored) "drip system" that has paid back its cost many times over. This "drip system" includes recipe cards, a birthday club letter (prearranged for clients to pick up a cake at their local bakery), monthly newsletters, anniversary cards for the settlement of their homes, and invitations to an annual night at their local ball game. Whether or not the client chooses to participate isn't important. Keeping my name in the forefront of their minds after the first contact is established is what's important. Later they'll know where to turn when my services are needed.

As this respondent observes, keeping one's eye on the purpose of business networking is a vital aspect of following up, too:

I've made several strong personal friendships with both men and women as a result of business networking. Like any relationship, they require work. It's been my experience, regardless of gender, that you need to be mindful of that when you reach that level of trust where it turns into a friendship, because then you can forget all about the business aspect of the relationship. This is why I feel it is key to have a structure in place that continually brings you back to generating business and making money. Losing sight of that changes the nature of the relationship.

♂ He Says . . .

Systems? We have systems for everything! Have you ever watched a man build a fire on the grill? It is a system of beauty. First you clean the grill, then you neatly stack the charcoals into a pyramid, and with great care then douse the charcoal with a precise amount of lighter fluid. Light that charcoal, and, ahhhh, fire. There's just something about fire! Once the fire is just right, as only a man can tell, it's time to throw your dinosaur steaks on the coals and let them sizzle! You see? We know systems, and the fire-making one is an example of one we perfected thousands of years ago.

There are many systems in business and it is important that we use them to our advantage, much like the fire. Putting systems in place that allow us to follow up consistently and stay in touch sounds like it should be pretty easy; after all, we dominated fire. So why do more men not use systems to complement their business activities? I would venture to say that staying in touch feels just a little too relational. After all, those business contacts already know us and we've already sold them something, so why do we need to stay in touch?

If I told you having a system would allow you to make more money, would you be willing to use one? Of course you would. More money equals more free time, and if systems are in place to help, then we save both time and effort.

How many times have you forgotten to follow up on a referral or a call in a timely manner? It probably wasn't because you didn't have every good intention of doing so, but sometimes we become so busy that we forget the little things. Yes, women are better natural multitaskers. We men have to put more systems into place to make sure that we don't drop that very detailed ball. Every time we do, it costs money! By and large, implementing more systems around our work allows us to make more money so that we have the time to do the things we love, like building fires!

 ## She Says . . .

The fortune is in the follow-up. Recently I passed a referral to a gentleman. I told him it was a done deal. I never heard from him, so I passed it to a second man and told him the same thing. He also never called me. The follow-up was completely dropped, simply because neither of these gentlemen had a system for following up, or there was an issue with me being a woman. Either way there was opportunity lost. This rarely happens to me with women, who will call or email me right away after a referral is made.

I once gave a man a $30,000 project referral that he never followed up on. I even called him a second time to give him a second chance. I gave the same referral to a woman and she followed up within 24 hours. Maybe this is the reason women feel they're getting more business from their networking activities than men. They are more consistent with follow-up.

The Survey Says . . .
Measuring Is Mandatory

If you track your networking efforts, you can study them and make sure they're giving you the return on your time investment. How much time do you spend per week on network activities? How much are you gaining for your business from this time investment? Measure average time and gains over a two-year period, then step back and assess your methods and production. Could you be doing things differently? If we are going to spend time doing anything in business, we must make sure it is giving us the return on our investment that we desire. What is the old saying? You can't manage it if you can't measure it. Ultimately, if you can measure it, you can see what's happening and change it.

 ## He Says . . .

It is all about ROI (return on investment) . . . right, guys? Time is money. Relationships are money. Time and relationships are money. If the time I am spending is not yielding me the correct amount of results, then that relationship HAS TO GO! How we men think: "The last thing I need is another 'relationship' with a man or a woman that goes nowhere . . . in terms of business. I need to know that my time is profitable. It is all about the bottom line, the ROI, the transaction . . . 'THE SALE!'"

Women, I am now going to show to you a formula that was given to us (men) before we went into the business world. Passed down from father to son, father to son . . . for generations. This is the first time it has ever been revealed to members of the opposite sex. This is our key to success over the last 500 billion years.

ROI Formula for Men

Sex of person x Age of person x Education x Years of experience
÷ Number of people in their network x The median of years of

relationship with each person – people under 32.5 years of age and people over 52.25 years of age.

When you have that number, then multiply it by 3.14666 and then convert to a fraction.

Once you have the fraction . . .

Please tell me you weren't actually doing this! You don't really think I am serious, do you?

The reality is, there is no mathematical formula for success when it comes to networking. As men, we like to think there is, but we have already pointed out in this book, sometimes we men (as a gender) are not the sharpest knives in the drawer.

So here is reality. Forget everything I said above the "Please tell me you weren't actually doing this!" Measuring our time, money, and energy investment is important. Measuring the actual results we are getting from our networking and referrals is important. I believe in it, I do. But, what is it that I am really measuring? Relationships are not possible to measure on paper. Networking results come from investing time and energy to a relationship. They develop through giving, caring, and wanting to help others. Let me ask you a couple of questions: Who is going to give you your next big referral? How much will it cost you and when will you receive it? I am pretty sure you cannot answer these questions. Why? Because YOU NEVER KNOW. You never know who is going to give you the next big referral.

The key to getting results from your networking associates, male and female, is the level of their sincerity in wanting to help you. What is the way to measure another's sincerity in helping you? Not sure, but that would be a cool formula.

We as men don't want to waste our time at events or with people who "don't get it." How do you know those people? You know. It is instinctive. (Unless of course you are one of those people who really don't get it or even get what I am saying here.) We have our life experience, our learned intelligence, our street knowledge, and our emotional intelligence that helps us to decide when a relationship is worthwhile to continue. Nobody can really teach us this. It comes from the inside.

Please make sure you are measuring the bottom line results you are getting from your various activities. Then step back and look at how you are investing into the relationships from those activities. I want you to look at each relationship and question whether it is worthwhile for your business and then look at it from their perspective. What ROI would you say are they getting from their relationship with you? Let's remember, your opinion on this does not matter. It is what they think and believe that matters to them. However, it needs to matter to you, because if they are not seeing you as a value asset and you are not seeing them as one, then the two of you have a great opportunity to develop a relationship that could end up being very beneficial to both of you.

Men, women are good at this part. We are to focused on the formula. The formula is nice, measuring is important, but the person, the relationship is what matters more. So, track and measure.

♀ She Says . . .

Time is often an in-demand commodity for most women. When we look at the statistics for the time spent networking between men and women, it comes as no surprise at all that men belong to more organizations, spend more time attending events, and on average spend more time per week networking than women do. Yet men state that they get less business from their networks than women do. Are men and women guessing about their time and results? Or do they actually have systems? In my work with hundreds of businessmen and women around this very topic, it is very rare that I find a man or a woman actually tracking their personal time and results.

One gentleman named Eric had an impeccable system around his activities and his results. He knew exactly how much time he was spending, what organizations were developing results for him, and how much money he made from each and every activity. In ten years, I have only met one person who actually could show me his system. Most of us just guess at our time spent and results, often estimating or guessing considerably over or under the actual.

If you a networking for your business, you have to measure your results. Time is money, and you cannot regain lost time. If I lost everything I have today, I know that given enough time I could recreate my wealth. The key is, would I have enough time? For women it always comes down to time, time for our family, time for work, time for friends, time for our self and others. To make the best use of our time we have to start by measuring our results.

I know, I know! I hear it all the time, you don't want to commercialize your networks, you don't want to seem pushy, you don't want to infringe upon the relationships. I just want to remind you that this is a book about business networking. Business requires measurements!

Measure Your Groups

- Make a list of all the groups that you are in right now.
- Ask yourself, why am I in this group and write down the reason.
- You have your list, now which of those groups still serve a purpose for you?
- How much business are you getting and how much are you giving to the people in those groups?
- Are you in groups just for support or did you intend to get and give referrals in the group?
- How long have you been a member of the group?

At the end of every year or before you decided to join another group, go through this process, and then decide what groups you are going to keep and which ones you are going to leave. **CAUTION**: Do not join groups, sit back and wait for things to happen, then walk away and say it did not work. You get out of any group what you are willing to put in. Take a look at yourself before you blame others or the group for your lack of referrals or business.

Here is a list of four things you should be measuring:

1. *Time*. How much time are you spending in the group or with individuals? A part of good networking is building good relationships. In the world of business networking we

build relationships that have a benefit to both sides. Building relationships take time; how much have you invested?

2. *Give.* How much business have you given to others? I cannot complain about not getting business from a referral source if I am not giving business from that referral source. It is important that you track the referrals you have given to others and what was the result of that referral.

3. *Receive.* How many referrals or leads have you received from the group or individual? This is key. What have you received from the group or the referral source over the past year? How many referrals or leads have I received from a person in my network or a referral source?

4. *Result.* How much money have you made as a result of the leads and referrals you have received? This relates to item 3, Receive. I get a lot of leads and referrals from people, but which of those are closing and which ones are not really very good? You may find out that the people you are giving good business to are only retuning low level leads to you.

If you find that you are not getting the results you expected from a group or a person, then take a look at what you may have communicated to them. Go back and decide if you have not been clear in your communications about what you want or need, or have you hit the wall with a taker who is happy to take your referrals, but not so forth coming when it is time to give you referrals.

Women often do not go through this process of measurement because it feels to calculating. It is infringing on the relationships. I beg to differ with all the women who have told me this; this is business networking. Measure your results and then you can manage your time. If you are not getting the results you want you can stop, reevaluate, and change course if you need to.

REMEMBER: If your network is not working, there is no business happening, and it is your fault. As long as you remember that it is your fault and you take full responsibility for it, then and only then, do you always have the capacity to change it. If you are not measuring you will never know if it is working or not.

Our time is limited ladies, and our three-ring circus calls upon us constantly, we must measure if we are going to make good use of our time.

The Survey Says ...
Effectiveness of Networking

We combined the answers to two questions to determine how effective a business tool networking actually is. One question asked how much time participants spent networking and the other asked what percentage of their business was derived from networking. Our analysis showed a linear correlation between the two factors. The more hours a person spent networking, the more business they derived from it. The correlation shown in Figure 8.1 is exactly that.

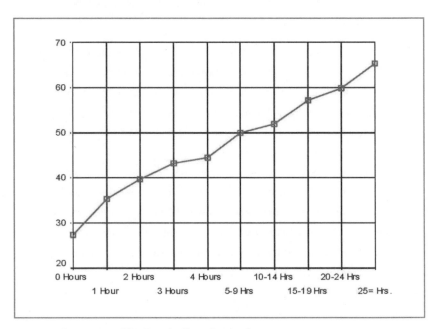

FIGURE 8.1—**Percentage of Business by Hours Invested**

Weekly Averages

It is important to note that the average (mean) weekly hours each survey participant spent on networking activities was 6.31. In other words, during a one-week period, people spent a little less than a full workday engaged in networking activities of some kind.

Interestingly, the majority of people who stated that networking did not play a role in their success (51.5 percent) spent two hours or less on networking! Clearly, those people who spent only a little time in the process felt that networking was not an effective way to build their businesses because just as in many other aspects of life, you reap what you sow. It's no wonder the people who didn't invest as much time also did not realize as much reward. This demonstrates the direct relationship between effort and rewards in networking.

The typical person in this survey generated 46.70 percent of all their business through referrals and networking activities. Men averaged 43.96 percent of their business through networking and referral activites and women averaged 49.44 percent of their business through networking and referral activities.

Quality Time Invested Returns Greater Rewards

This last set of data is very interesting. We found that out of the 12,000 global participants, women spent less time networking (6.19 hours compared to 6.44 for men), yet generated a higher percentage of their business through the process (49.44 percent compared to 43.96 percent for men).

The quote below supports the power of following up as a productive technique for getting maximum results within time constraints, since women gain more business without investing as much networking time.

In most groups, I find that only a small number of people are prepared to network and follow up properly. Women are much better at following up. My mentor taught me well when he said that the fortune is in the follow-up.

Why would women spend less time and get a higher percentage of their business from referrals than men? This is a question that puzzled us a great deal. I'm afraid we have more questions than we do answers about this particular issue.

Since women tend to be more "relational," based on the survey findings, are they networking without thinking of it as "networking"? In other words, are they actually networking when they feel they are socializing without a business purpose?

Women have often told me that they are responsible for more things that men are, such as child care and various household responsibilities. Consequently, are they more focused in the limited time they have for networking than men are? Are they just being more productive because they have less time? I really can't say, but it is a question worth investigating.

Neither of these questions are answered in the data, and I am not suggesting that these ideas are true. They are simply posed as questions. Why do women spend less time networking and yet claim a higher percentage of business through referrals than men?

Here—the data is clear. They do both.

♂ He Says . . .

We men spend more time and get fewer results. That's not good any way you look at it. Why would that be? Fault lies either in our technique, knowledge, or practical application; or possibly all three. Maybe it's a good ol' boy thing. We go out to network with our buddies and spend time hanging out together, but not meeting any new people. We are doing business with our "buds" but aren't doing "more" business with our buds.

Here's what really confuses me. We've found that men are results-oriented and very focused on transactions over relationships. If that's true, if we are all about the results of the transactions and women are not as focused on the transaction, sale, or results, then why are they creating more business in less time? Is it me, or does this also make us look like idiots?

　　　　　　　8 / Planned Systems Yield More Results

The short answer is that people want to do business with people they know, trust, and like. They want to give their money to those they feel most confident in. If I don't know or trust you, it just isn't going to happen.

Men, I think we need to learn from the women here about focusing on quality, rather than quantity time. No surprise there!

She Says . . .

Time is more often in greater demand for women than men, because of their balancing act between family and profession, so they rein in their formal networking hours to accommodate those demands. When we examine the statistics, it comes as no surprise that men belong to more organizations, spend more time attending related events, and on average also spend more time per week networking than women do, yet report less business as a result of working their networks than women do.

Since their time is limited, it is mandatory that women make tidy use of the time they do allot for networking, leveraging their efforts to maximum potential. Men in general have more time to network and connect with others in the business world, so women need to produce more results in less time to compete effectively with them.

WHAT'S OLD IS NEW AGAIN: SHOP-A-HOLIC ALERT

Have you ever shined up a pair of very good shoes you'd forgotten about and been impressed by how lovely they are? Sometimes a quality current or even old connection can work the same way with some attention, nurturing, and of course, buffing. Don't forget about the "shoes" already in your closet and become an unsatisfied shop-a-holic with a closet full of many, but shallow connections (cheap shoes).

Our study shows that the more time a person spends networking, the more successful they are. Therefore, if the hours a woman can work are limited by her lifestyle, it follows that her potential for results would be limited also. Her only alternative is to find better ways to utilize the time she has, choosing groups that fit her family life. Necessity is the mother of invention, right? Predominately, women in this predicament have chosen groups that meet midday since mornings and evenings are traditionally family social time reserved for attending to kids out of school, household obligations, mealtimes, etc.

Most business professionals spend a lot of time running from one networking event to the next, meeting more new people in hopes that they'll sell a product or service to someone in the room. This time-sucker becomes frustrating to women when their ambitious intentions position them behind the eight ball, partially because they cannot make it to as many meetings as they feel would be appropriate to fuel their business with. Contrary to this frustration, when women focus on quality over quantity networking they find their double lives as busy moms and business owners can work together and produce positive business results.

THE TORTOISE AND THE HARE

Women take the slower, steady path to networking, stopping along the way to invest time in building their relationships, while men sprint the mad dash straight to getting business fast by skipping some of the developmental, middle steps in networking. At the finish line, men seem to have a quicker return for their time, but it is the women who are winning the race, breaking through the ribbon with deeper, and more fruitful, connections.

Potent networking requires planning. It's important to stay organized with your time and decide which groups you'll get involved with and how much time you'll allow for each of them. Keeping a dedicated calendar to parse time, just like with a financial budget, helps keep time expenditures on track. This kind of organization seems to allow most of us women to manage our options. Women are very adept at juggling calendars with multiple priorities on it.

The next step after budgeting time is to set goals to accomplish in our groups. This requires follow-up time post events, which we also budget for.

The more systems we "install" into our networking credo, the more success we'll generate with limited time. Most people know vast numbers of other people, but actually spend a lot of their time trying to meet even more new people, thinking ever larger numbers of acquaintances will be good for their careers, but we know now how that is not the most productive use of our time.

Most of us remember the caution from our parents to choose a few things and do them very well, rather than only being a little skilled at many things. Relationships work the same way!

We are far better off concentrating on adding people to our networks systematically, limiting the system to numbers we can manage in a quality way. Allowing us to do what we have always done for our families, remembering birthdays, anniversaries, and other important relational information about our network.

Speaking to quality, people are far better off concentrating on adding people to their networks systematically, limiting the system to numbers they can manage in a quality way. Ask yourself if you can remember the birthdays, family members' names, hobbies, previous conversations, and life desires of the number of people you currently are socializing with. If the answer is no, it's time to get more organized, assess your numbers, and step up the quality in your relationships with people already connected to you.

The Survey Says...
The Connection Between Tracking and Success

The old saying that we "treasure what we measure"—and vice versa— turns out to be highly relevant in networking. As we explored the extent to which survey respondents correlated success and networking, we discovered that most of the people who credit networking for some of their success also maintain a system for measuring the dollar value of their networking activity. Conversely, most of the respondents who said networking played no role in their success had no system for tracking any money generated by their participation in networking groups.

In a world where news media frequently reports the latest sports scores, stock market numbers, and even the weekend's top-grossing

Do you have a system to track any money that you generate from your participation in networking groups?			
	Has networking played a role in your success?		
	Yes	No	Response Totals
Yes, I have a current system	53.0% (5,408)	34.4% (205)	51.9% (5,613)
No, I currently do not have a system	47.0% (4,803)	65.6% (391)	48.1% (5,194)
Answered questions	10,210	596	10,806
Skipped question			1,198

FIGURE 8.2—**Tracking Financial Success by Using a System**

films, wouldn't you think common sense would motivate business networkers to track how much they're making from their efforts? Unfortunately, common sense isn't all that common.

High-performance professional networking requires the same attention to success metrics as a pro athlete, stockbroker, or even the local cineplex. Why? We can affect what we can measure by changing what we do. In other words, what we can measure, we can change. After analysis, our world can be shaped to how we want it to be—successful. Figure 8.2 shows a proven example of this truth.

Track Your Garden, Watch It Grow

How do you keep track of the birthdays, anniversaries, and other important events in your life? Most likely, you use some sort of calendar—something as simple as a wall-hanger or as sophisticated as the newest day planner. In other words, you use a system—whatever works best for you.

More importantly, why do you use any sort of calendar system? Because those birthdays, anniversaries, and other important events are also important to the people in your life. You value your relationship with your spouse, so you keep your eye on your anniversary date. You value your relationships with family and friends, so you keep track of their birthdays.

Long-term relationships are at the core of networking, as well. Our survey respondents who believed that they should focus on building a relationship with someone before trying to do business with that person also indicated they have a system for tracking the dollar value of their networking. The system actually helps them focus on and nurture the relationship—and understand its business value over the long run.

Interestingly, most of the respondents who preferred a transactional approach to networking, (hit 'em up for business now and worry about the relationship later or never), used no system to track the money generated by their networking. They not only failed to focus on the relationship as one of primary importance, but they also didn't pay attention to whether their networking was financially productive. Isn't that a bit like saying maybe you'll remember some of the birthdays in your life if you're not too busy or distracted at the time, but either way it's no big deal? Really?

Both Genders Benefit From Tracking

Attaching a system to your networking is key to creating more success for the time that you have to spend. Most networkers are out there just meeting people and adding to their networks but have not fully engaged the network that they have already developed nor are they tracking the activities or the results they generate.

Here is what Dr. Herminia Ibarra, INSEAD University Professor of Organisational Behaviour, had to say about going deeper into your network:

> *It's the quality not the quantity of contacts and how you use them that really counts. Managers need to remember that networking is a two-way street, and they need to offer help and make connections for others in their network as well as expecting help from them. You can have the biggest contact list in your field, but if you only pick up the phone when you are in a crisis, you won't get far. That's why you don't want to leave yourself vulnerable to having nowhere to turn when you do have a crisis. Relationships take time, effort, and they each have their own rhythm. Depending on what you put in, what you give back to it, and to the extent you invest in it for the future, your network will be there for you.*

That which gets tracked, gets done. When you track your activities consistently you understand where your successes occur and therefore where your time and energy is best invested.

♂ He Says . . .
Tracking Is All About Systems

As we have previously discussed, one of the most important things that you can do for your business is to create systems around everything you do. The more efficient systems you have in place, the more likely you are to be able to sell your business for a profit, create greater wealth, and predict your annual growth with regularity. Question: Why do we men like systems so much? Answer: Multitasking! We know from earlier in this book that a man's brain is not set up as well as a woman's to multitask. This means, if men don't have systems to remember and make things happen, we will forget whatever it is we are supposed to do. Ladies, stop nodding and smiling. We know you know this, we just can't let you know that we know this about ourselves too. This is why anniversaries and birthdays get missed by us on a regular basis. We are simple creatures. Multitasking for me means watching my favorite sport on TV, drinking a beer with my left hand, and having chips ready to go with my right without having to look away from a 52-inch screen. Much easier said than done. Trust me.

Creating systems around your network and referrals is no different. If you are going to spend your time networking, meeting people, collecting business cards, getting and giving referrals, then putting systems in place will allow you to do it with greater ease and success. I am always amazed when I take on a new client and we start talking about their database system—the very core of their network—and nine out of ten times they will bring out a shoebox full of business cards. (By the way, a shoebox was a technological improvement over my second desk drawer, which also held my stapler, tape dispenser, and paper clips.)

Here are some tips with which to build a basic system:

- *Use a database*. Having a database with all your contacts is key to growing a good network. I once sat down with a referral partner to survey and mine each other's databases. He went through mine and identified everyone he wanted to meet. When it was my turn to go through his, he brought out the shoebox. Who do you think got value out of that activity?

The database should be sorted into functional categories. Identify the people in it by visibility, credibility, or profitability. Having a good database or CRM is key to your success when you are developing your network.

- *Create a post-event follow-up method.* Develop a system for follow-up after networking events. This is so important that you should allow a full day after your networking event to do all the follow up. You must also put a follow-up priority system in place. Who do you follow-up with first? As men, being the transaction-type animals we are, our first priority will be to follow up with those with whom we think we can do business. I am not saying that is what should be done, just what is done. This would be a good place for me to say: Men, don't put all your efforts into those who you think will be the most immediate clients. Ever hear the term, penny wise, dollar foolish? This would be an example of that. By not following up in a timely manner with those people who could be great referral sources for you and you for them, you end up going for the immediate money only. Meanwhile, you are letting all your pipeline business get away. Your network is not just about "today's money" but can really help you with "tomorrow's money." This is one of the biggest problems we have as small-business owners and sales professionals. We tend to not work on enough of "tomorrow's money" and therefore we are always working on bringing in the business we need now, which can get tiring and very stressful. By setting a focused follow-up plan in place you can get results for both your short- and long-term sales.

- *Track your results.* Where is your business coming from? Who is passing you referrals? What organizations are the most productive for you to put your time into? If you are not tracking your results, then you don't have any idea where your time is best spent to make money. If you have one or two people who are consistently sending you business, it would be wise for you to invest more time in those people rather than using your time to meet new people. Without tracking, there is no way to know where your results are coming from. One company started tracking all their business and found that it was not the salespeople who were bringing in the most business. It was the receptionist! Don't you think it might be important that this person be recognized for her efforts?

- *Practice a thank-you courtesy.* Please. Thank you. Excuse me. Didn't we learn this in kindergarten? These three phrases make the difference between the civilized world and the noncivilized world . . . at least in my opinion. I want you to think of the people who are your networking associates not as friends or family, but as your most valued client. If your most valued client gave you a referral, what would you do? 1) Thank them at the moment they gave it to you. 2) Contact that person right away to show you truly appreciated the referral. 3) Communicate back with your top client to let them know that you had spoken to Mrs. Referral and what the current status is. 4) Treat Mrs. Referral like gold, because it came from your best client. 5) Inform Mr. Best Client of the final result. 6) Send Mr. Best Client a thank-you card or gift to show your appreciation for the referral. Yes? Is this a rough draft of the follow-up plan you would put in place? Of course! Why? Because they are your best client. You don't want them mad at you. You want them to see how serious you take the referral and how much you truly appreciate their trust, confidence, and energy. And, the selfish reason—you would like more referrals from them.

If you have committed networking associates, THEY ARE YOUR MR. & MRS. BEST CLIENTS. They are willing to refer your business over and over, if you do the right thing. So, do the right thing. Say thank you every time you get a referral and follow the process above. The thank you is important, but keeping them informed is even more important.

I cannot tell you how many times I've given referrals to people and then never heard from them again. I love when people get back to me and tell me how great the referral worked out. It makes me feel good knowing that I was able to help a friend. It also makes me feel great to be appreciated. People love to be recognized for the things they do.

• *Track your time.* Time is money. How much time are you putting into your efforts? Are you making the appropriate amount of return on the time invested? How will you know the answer to that if you aren't tracking your time?

If you take the time to implement systems around your networking activities, you will find that you get better results but, it will also allow you more time to do the other things that your personal three-ring circus requires of you. During the year you may have more time to attend events than other times. Even though you may not be able to network as much as you would like or feel you need to, you can keep in touch with your associates by putting touch point systems in place. These are time-savers. Sending cards out on a regular basis: Schedule it on your calendar. I have the birthdays of all my family members on my calendar. Not very impressive . . . but wait, there is more. I also have scheduled to send a card in the mail to them seven days ahead of time. Are you impressed yet? There's more. I also have scheduled a shopping day to get the card one week before the day I need to send the card out. (No, not a whole day . . . but you know what I mean.) C'mon . . . you ladies are definitely impressed now. Just admit it. Men are actually in shock and can't imagine ever putting this much time, energy, or organization into birthdays. Men tend to specialize in belated birthday cards. Why do I do this? Time. I am very busy. If I don't manage my time I will never finish what I need to.

Consider the investment of your time in networking as part of your marketing budget. Networking is about building relationships for future mutual benefit. It is a marketing activity. By putting your time into the marketing budget, you start to understand the importance of tracking because it now becomes part of the bottom line number you have to go after in order to be profitable.

- *Go deep, not wide.* I am sure you have heard over the years about how the TV and movie stars splayed on the covers of all the magazines and out with many people in the public eye tend to be home alone a lot. There are many people who network like this. They become very well known but have no real relationships with anyone in their network. So they have achieved their personal level of fame but they are not seeing any real benefit from it except being popular when they go out. We must be focused on developing the relationships in the network, not the size of our networks. Yes, men . . . you must be developing the actual RELATIONSHIP with the people in your network. It is important that we work in our network and not just on our network. Chances are you already know just about everyone you need to know to build a successful referral business, but you have not devoted enough time to go deep into your network. They say the average businessperson's network consists of about 225 contacts—people they actually know and have some type of positive relationship with. So if you have about 225 people in your network and each of them have 225 people in their network, that means you are one generation away from a little over 50,000 people. How many more people did you say you wanted to meet? Always growing your network is great, but spend a greater amount of time developing the relationships you currently have but are at a shallow level. Automating your network with a database system will allow you to spend time working in your network, building deeper relationships. Good systems will allow you to do just that—go deep into you network.
- *Manage your social media.* Dedicate time to updating and managing your Twitter, Facebook, and LinkedIn accounts (or whatever platforms you use), and to create fresh, interesting

content for your blog. These are great ways to stay in touch with your network, develop conversation with them, and find out what they need.

One of my clients got seven new accounts by paying close attention to his Facebook page. His business focuses on disaster recovery, and during a time when damaging storms were raging across the state, he watched his Facebook page to see what his network was saying. He simply asked how he could be of help, and seven people hired him to help recover their homes.

♀ She Says . . .
Systems Make a Difference

Of the 12,000 people surveyed, more respondents said they did not have a system than said they did have a system. More importantly, women said no, they did not have a system to follow up more than men did! It is easy to see that the more systematic you learn to make your networking the more productive you are going to be. Male or female, having a system is key to success. For women this can really be a major key for them.

Women have fewer hours to actually spend networking. They have to balance family responsibilities from getting kids off to school in the morning to getting them to their after-school activities, home for dinner, and off to bed. Add to that all the other activities that they need to take care of in a given day and there is little time for networking. Having systems to follow up and stay in touch allows for more productive activities and results from your networking activities.

When we asked the questions: Do you have a system for follow-up? Do you track the business you get from networking? Do you have a system for staying in touch? Men and women were consistently close to one another.

Overall, more people said they did not have systems versus those that did. Having systems to do all these activities are key for men and women.

There is no way to create success if your success is out in "airy-fairy" land. Hard facts and data tell you what you are doing well and what you are not doing at all. Tracking is a key factor in success.

BNI is an excellent example of this point. A good BNI chapter tracks everything from attendance, referrals passed, referrals received, and dollars generated, and they track this for each and every member in the chapter. The most successful members and the most successful chapters are the ones who track consistently and review those results regularly.

My Referral Institute clients spend a lot of time reviewing in class their activities from the week prior. They keep networking score cards that let them know what activities they are doing and with whom and what results they are getting and from whom. If they do not track they have no way of knowing who is referring them, who they have given referrals to, and what activities and organizations are paying off for them.

There is a saying, "What gets tracked, gets done." Nothing could be more true. Men and women alike take networking as a casual activity, they go to events, meet people, gather cards, and go back to the office. For most people it ends there. Organizations like BNI and some other groups have systems in place during the meeting, but if the members of those types of organizations do not have a system in place after they leave the meeting, they will have less success than those who do develop a system for their networks.

Track Everything

There are so many things that need to be tracked:

- What organizations you belong to and what results you are getting from them?
- How much time are you spending networking and working your network?
- How much money have you made as a result of your activities?

- Who is sending you referrals, and how much of your income are they responsible for?

You must have systems around all the tracking as well as systems for:

- Following up with those people you meet
- Staying in touch with your network members
- Rewarding your referral sources
- How you are going to help your referral sources

Ladies, here is the key for you to understand: If you learn to use good systems, it will allow you to get better results in much less time. This will free up more of your time for family and personal life. The work and time is upfront developing and implementing the system. On the backside you will spend much less time going out networking and more time working in your network. For most of us, we already know all the people we need to know to make a living. We don't need to keep adding people to our network—we need to get into our network and start developing it.

Your Best Networking Self

The Survey Says...
Our Findings Distilled

What have 12,000 surveys, almost 1,000 comments and stories, numerous interviews, months of research, and years of experience allowed us to conclude? Below is a recap of the facts we uncovered, and we think it will help to keep these in mind as you follow the advice of He and She, as logic behind your new habits.

Study Findings, Summarized

- Men and women were closer together than we expected in most areas.
- However, the perception of the difference is very dramatic. Remember: The exception becomes the perception.

- Women feel that networking has played a slightly larger role in their success than men.
- Women use a much wider variety of techniques to learn their networking skills than men do.
- Men are more likely to focus on business first than women are. Women are a little more likely to focus on building the relationship first—then the business.
- The time of day for networking was not a big issue for either gender. This was a surprise to us.
- Family obligations were more of a problem for women.
- Women definitely did not feel as safe as men in attending evening events.
- Men preferred either structured or an unstructured networking event. Women felt OK with either.
- Both men and women felt that other people were more uncomfortable networking than they felt about it themselves.
- Men felt stronger about transactional aspects of networking. Women felt stronger about relational aspects of networking.
- Men spent a little more time networking.
- Women received a higher percentage of the business from networking than men.
- The more time either men or women spent in their networking efforts, the higher the percentage of business they generated.
- The more often people used systems to track their business from networking, the more likely they were to feel that networking played a role in their success.

Men and women are not so different in the success they desire in business and networking. However the process, the mindset, and the way of making the results happen are very different. The reason is that we have different ways of viewing the world. Some of this comes from nature and some from nurture. What it means is that if we want to be more effective, we must learn how to respect, appreciate, and embrace one another's differences. We must understand that we can work more effectively together as a team in business and in our networks. We just need to learn to be adaptable, empathetic, sensitive, and understanding that THEY are not you.

You can and will beat the odds. The exception doesn't have to become the perception. It can be you!

Here is some parting advice from the whole team to take with you into your brightest future potential for networking success.

We Say . . .

We're all trying to get to the same place. It will be much more profitable for all of us if we can help each other along the way. Here are a few things to guide your success in networking with the complementary gender:

For the Ladies

- Don't get stuck in the credibility phase of the VCP Process®. Ask for what you want.
- When asking for help, communicate clearly exactly what it is that you want.
- Make time for networking.
- When speaking to men try to impress them and share your accomplishments.
- When spoken to inappropriately, speak up about it immediately.

For the Guys

- Slow down and build the relationship.
- Work through the VCP Process® in the proper order of its phases. Don't race through the credibility phase.
- Make and maintain eye contact.
- Listen and ask relational questions.
- Don't assume that women don't take their businesses seriously.
- Don't hit on women at networking events.

For the Ladies

- Dress for business at business events.
- Put systems in place to track your business.
- Stay in contact with and follow up on leads, referrals, and acquaintances made.
- Diversify your networks.
- Remember that networking is ultimately about getting business, so ask for both business and referrals.
- Convey an image to others that you are a serious businessperson, in all that you do.
- Get educated about referral systems.
- Don't lump all men into the same group.

For the Guys

- Edit what you are about to say, using filters to sift out what is not business appropriate.
- Stay in contact with and follow up on leads, referrals, and acquaintances made.
- Stay informed about the best, most current, and cutting-edge networking practices.
- Develop and use systems for your networking activities.
- Make time for networking.
- Speak to relate not just to impress.
- Remember that women are at networking events for business gain, just as you are.

The difference between us is a great advantage, not a disadvantage. By following the steps we have outlined in this book, you should be able to develop a more productive relationship with members of both sexes. As we bid you adieu, we send you off into the complex blue yonder of coed professional networking with gender-specific simplified checklists.

Good luck, and stay tuned to BusinessNetworkingandSex.com for the latest developments in business networking AND sex!

Index